Writing in Social Spaces

Writing in Social Spaces addresses the problem of making time and space for writing in the academic life and work of the professionals and practitioners who do academic writing. Even those who want to write, who know how to write well and who have quality publications report that they cannot find enough time for writing. Many supervisors are unsure about how to help postgraduates improve their writing for thesis and publication. While the problem does present through concerns with 'time', it is also partly about writing practices, academic identities and lack of motivation.

This book provides a research-based, theorised approach to the skill of writing while retaining a link to writing practices and giving immediate yet sustainable solutions to the writing problem.

It supplies new theory and practice on:

- socialising writing-in-progress and writing with others;
- exploring the alternation of conscious and unconscious, internal and external processes in academic writing while in a social grouping;
- applying social processes in the writing process.

Using case studies and vignettes of writing in social spaces to illustrate the theory in practice, this book is a valuable resource for academics, scholars, professionals and practitioners, as well as researchers at all stages of their career, and in all disciplines.

Rowena Murray is Professor in Education, University of the West of Scotland, UK.

The Society for Research into Higher Education (SRHE) is an independent and financially self-supporting international learned Society. It is concerned to advance understanding of higher education, especially through the insights, perspectives and knowledge offered by systematic research and scholarship.

The Society's primary role is to improve the quality of higher education through facilitating knowledge exchange, discourse and publication of research. SRHE members are worldwide and the Society is an NGO in operational relations with UNESCO.

The Society has a wide set of aims and objectives. Amongst its many activities the Society:

• is a specialist publisher of higher education research, journals and books, amongst them Studies in Higher Education, Higher Education Quarterly, Research into Higher Education Abstracts and a long running monograph book series.

The Society also publishes a number of in-house guides and produces a specialist series "Issues in Postgraduate Education".

• funds and supports a large number of special interest networks for researchers and practitioners working in higher education from every discipline. These networks are open to all and offer a range of topical seminars, workshops and other events throughout the year ensuring the Society is in touch with all current research knowledge.

• runs the largest annual UK-based higher education research conference and parallel conference for postgraduate and newer researchers. This is attended by researchers from over 35 countries and showcases current research across every aspect of higher education.

SRHE *Society for Research into Higher Education*
Advancing knowledge Informing policy Enhancing practice

73 Collier Street
London N1 9BE
United Kingdom

T +44 (0)20 7427 2350
F +44 (0)20 7278 1135
E srheoffice@srhe.ac.uk

www.srhe.ac.uk

Director: Helen Perkins
Registered Charity No.313850
Company No. 00868820
Limited by Guarantee
Registered office as above

Society for Research into Higher Education (SRHE) series

Series Editors: Jennifer M. Case, University of Cape Town
Jeroen Huisman, University of Ghent

Published titles:
Intellectual Leadership in Higher Education: Renewing the Role of the University Professor
Bruce Macfarlane

Strategic Curriculum Change: Global Trends in Universities
Paul Blackmore and Camille B. Kandiko

Reconstructing Identities in Higher Education: The Rise of 'Third Space' Professionals
Celia Whitchurch

The University in Dissent: Scholarship in the Corporate University
Gary Rolfe

Everything for Sale? The Marketisation of UK Higher Education
Roger Brown with Helen Carasso

Literacy in the Digital University: Critical Perspectives on Learning, Scholarship and Technology
Robin Goodfellow and Mary R. Lea

Researching Student Learning in Higher Education: A Social Realist Approach
Jennifer M. Case

Women Leaders in Higher Education: Shattering the Myths
Tanya Fitzgerald

Digital Technology and the Contemporary University: Degrees of Digitization
Neil Selwyn

Writing in Social Spaces

A social processes approach to academic writing

Rowena Murray

 Routledge
Taylor & Francis Group

LONDON AND NEW YORK

First published 2015
by Routledge
2 Park Square, Milton Park, Abingdon, Oxon OX14 4RN
together with the Society for Research into Higher Education
73 Collier Street London N1 9BE UK

and by Routledge
711 Third Avenue, New York, NY 10017
together with the Society for Research into Higher Education
73 Collier Street London N1 9BE UK

Routledge is an imprint of the Taylor & Francis Group, an informa business

British Library Cataloguing in Publication Data
A catalogue record for this book is available from the British Library

Library of Congress Cataloging in Publication Data
A catalog record for this book has been requested

ISBN: 978-0-415-82870-3 (hbk)
ISBN: 978-0-415-82871-0 (pbk)
ISBN: 978-1-315-75542-7 (ebk)

Typeset in Galliard
by Swales & Willis Ltd, Exeter, Devon, UK

This book is dedicated to people who want to write more and would like to be able to enjoy it more.

Contents

Illustrations

Figures

Tables

Series editors' introduction

This series, co-published by the Society for Research into Higher Education and Routledge Books, aims to provide, in an accessible manner, cutting-edge scholarly thinking and inquiry that reflects the rapidly changing world of higher education, examined in a global context.

Encompassing topics of wide international relevance, the series includes every aspect of the international higher education research agenda, from strategic policy formulation and impact to pragmatic advice on best practice in the field. Each book in the series aims to meet at least one of the principle aims of the Society: to advance knowledge; to enhance practice; to inform policy.

Academic writing is often portrayed as a 'secret act', in that academics not easily share and discuss their writing practices. Rowena Murray argues for a perspective on writing as a social activity. The book addresses – on the basis of conceptual and theoretical work rooted in e.g. containment theory, and on Rowena's impressive experience – various aspects of and challenges in the writing process. The book ultimately aims to make writing more manageable and meaningful.

Jennifer M. Case
Jeroen Huisman

Acknowledgements

I would like to thank the following for providing funding to support the research that underpins this book:

British Academy:

'An evaluation of writers' retreats for academics' (BA44903, 2007).

- Presented at Society for Research in to Higher Education Annual Conference (SRHE), 2007; Writing Development in Higher Education Conference (WDHE), 2008, Keynote; and British Educational Research Association Annual Conference (BERA), 2009 and 2010 (Murray, 2007b, 2008d; MacLeod et al. 2009; Murray et al. 2010).
- Published in *Studies in Higher Education* (MacLeod *et al.* 2012) *Higher Education Research and Development* (Murray and Newton 2009) and *British Educational Research Journal* (Murray *et al.* 2012).

Nuffield Foundation:

1 'Identifying the mechanisms involved in scholarly publication' (2005)
   o Presented at SRHE 2006 and WDHE 2008 Keynote (Murray 2006, 2008d).
   o Published in *British Educational Research Journal* (Murray 2012).
2 'The Writing Consultation: A novel mechanism to develop academic writing practices' (SGS/37480, 2009).
   o Presented at WDHE 2010 and BERA 2011 (Murray 2010b, 2011a).
   o Published in *Higher Education Research and Development* (Murray and Thow forthcoming).

University of Strathclyde:

1   'Writing for publication: A pilot study to define practices, strategies and outputs following participation in a writer's group (RDF1433, 2007)
    o   Presented at BERA 2008; Improving University Teaching Conference 2008; WDHE 2008, Keynote; and SRHE 2012 (Murray 2008b, 2008c, 2008d, 2012c).
    o   Published in *South African Journal of Higher Education* (Murray 2007).
2   'Engagement with academic writing/disengagement from other tasks: A scoping study' (RDF1684, 2010).
    o   Presented at BERA 2011, SRHE 2011 and WDHE 2012 (Murray 2010b, 2011c, 2012b).
    o   Published in *Higher Education* (Murray 2013a).

I would like to thank the anonymous reviewers of my proposal for this book for their comments and suggestions. They would probably rather have been getting on with their own writing than reviewing mine, so I appreciate their time and effort.

Many people listened to me talking about this book, and I can't thank them enough for their generous attention and stimulating discussions. Thank you everyone who gave me feedback on draft chapters. I should add that as I name people here, it's not to blame them for any errors I make in this book, but to make my thanks a bit more personal. So, thank you Matthew Alexander, Trish Cain, Morag Findlay, Magnus George, Jim Hartley, Fiona Hay, Helena Kettleborough, Laura Steckley, Morag Thow and Mary Welsh.

Last, but by no means least – thanks to the Black Bull Hotel in Gartmore, where most of this book was written at retreats, to Liz and Andy and all the staff and to every retreat participant who asked me how my book was going, when they would probably rather have been talking about their own writing. I'm kidding – it's always been a two-way thing. Thank you all for making our retreats fun and productive.

Introduction
Making writing relational

My back story

More than twenty years ago I started to do research in academic writing while I was running writing workshops for PhD students, academics and professionals. At that time there seemed to be an expectation that everyone should know all they need to know about writing and just get on with it, but the experience of people who came to my writing workshops suggested otherwise. Writing triggered acute anxiety for many students, academics and professionals, and I wanted to help.

I had always been interested in writing – it is so complex, so daunting and so important in so many ways: for demonstrating learning, or as a mechanism for learning, for career progression, clarifying thinking, creating new knowledge – there's a seemingly endless list of writing's functions, processes, practices and potential in both educational and work settings. Writing is also so personal – so much of ourselves is invested in our writing.

At first, I drew on my experience of teaching Rhetoric and Composition at the Pennsylvania State University. Why did we not do any of this in the UK, I wondered? I started to adapt materials and activities we had used there, such as freewriting, rhetorical modes and the mechanics of writing. I developed new thesis writing courses, supported students in hundreds of one-to-one sessions and then started to support academics and professionals in courses on writing and publication.

Over the years, I created several new ways of developing and supporting academic writing – writing groups, retreats, courses and workshops. These all helped participants, but there were still barriers, and the barrier they found most difficult to overcome, they said, was a lack of time for writing.

While I had started out by focusing on individual writing skills, I began to focus more on the role of group writing activities, looking at writing development in terms of the social processes that develop writing skills. I began to see connections between outputs and relationships. I wondered if writing could be both personal and social, and started to research the role of social processes in the development of writing skills and our ability to deploy these skills. I ran a number of research projects to explore this idea and published several articles and wove these ideas into my books.

This book draws on all of this development work and all of these studies. It defines and illustrates the role of social writing with quotations from interviews with writers in professional and academic settings. My aim is to explain the social components of writing and to show how it can help writers address the many challenges of writing – including making time to write – and find meaning, pleasure and satisfaction in their academic writing.

No one talks about writing

> It's like a secret activity . . . No one else in my department talks about writing practices. They all present themselves as over pressured and far too busy to write . . . This can't be the case as they are all publishing, but writing practice is denied and not shared.

This is the view of an experienced, successful and published academic in what is generally considered a 'good' UK university. It shows that while writing is a social act, in the sense that it is socially constructed, and when we write we are influenced by the society of writing around us, it is not generally discussed in these terms. In some settings it is not discussed at all – it is the very opposite of 'social' in that sense. This is paradoxical: a social process that is practised without the use of social processes?

Moreover, when the process of writing is 'secret', 'denied' or 'not shared' it can be difficult to build the skills, networks and habits required for writing. It can be impossible to find out what writing involves, how writers develop and how the writing process may be managed in relation to other tasks. This, in turn, may inhibit the development of academics, researchers or practitioners who have to – and want to – produce and publish writing.

This book explores the potential for social groupings to impact on our writing. Since writing is implicated in our social positioning in academic and other communities, it is important – and intriguing – to look at the social processes involved and to think about whether or not we can embed those processes in our writing practices.

In many settings, making writing social is not the norm. Talking about writing is not the norm. Writing with others is not the norm. Yet, if writing is never discussed, how can it be relational? Of course, we talk about 'writing' in terms of outputs, but not so much about the process of producing these outputs and all the stages along the way, and these stages do not generally involve talking about the specifics of writing practices – what do we actually do when we write?

As long as it is a 'secret activity' it is difficult to be clear about what exactly writing is. In fact, as long as writing is 'denied', there is, in some settings, a stigma attached to discussing writing. Those who want to discuss writing risk being seen as – or worry about being seen as – weak, in need of remedial help, rather than as exchanging knowledge and expertise about the content and process of this important component of research. This stigma will, in turn, inhibit discussion: why do you need to talk about your writing? – just get on with it.

Social writing addresses these challenges. It can work in spite of this stigma. For many, it is immediately helpful – and interesting, literally thought provoking – to talk about writing and, in a sense, build talking into writing. This is helpful not just in the sense of providing relief or camaraderie, as in 'It's good to know we are all in the same boat' – which is *not* always a relief in any case – but in the sense of providing alternative, productive strategies and sustaining productive writing habits in communities of writers. Social writing means establishing a sense of community, being part of a community of scholars, and it lets us rehearse our writing in safe but rigorous conversations.

The aim of this book is therefore not just to get more people into print, or to get those who already publish to write even more – although these are valuable and important outcomes of social writing. Instead, it aims to make writing more manageable and meaningful for academics, researchers and professionals and thereby increase writing and improve people's experiences of writing. Social writing is, above all, about creating conversations around productivity, that are specific to participants' writing projects. It's about talking about what we want to write.

Overview of this book

Chapter 1 explains what making writing 'social' means, what it involves and why it is a good idea.

Chapter 2 deals with the first form of social writing I developed – writer's group: my experience of running lots of groups in different settings has helped to explain – for me and for participants – what exactly people do, think and feel when they write. Our writer's group discussions exposed different writing processes and helped us understand issues we had with writing. This chapter explains how these issues can be addressed and resolved in writing groups.

Chapter 3 describes a formal, credit-bearing course on academic writing that I developed and taught for academics and researchers. In this course, students read selected literature on academic writing – a new field for most participants – and learned about different approaches to doing and researching academic writing. This chapter argues that delving into the extensive literature on academic writing – covering the spectrum from the practical, 'how to write' to the theoretical – can have benefit for academics and professionals, not only for their own writing but also for how they use writing activities in their teaching and supervision. It explains how these advanced seminars increased their understanding, changed their writing habits (with some exceptions) and stimulated their writing.

Chapter 4 explains how I incorporated social writing activities in workshops. It describes an integrated strategy for writing that combines different modes of writing to create productive practices. It explains how discussion at stages in the writing process exposes participants' issues, increases their understanding of writing and of themselves as writers and offers alternative models for writing.

Chapter 5 describes a form of writing retreat I designed: the structured writing retreat that develops the habit of social writing which, in turn, increases both the time available for writing and participants' written outputs. It explains how these retreats not only provide social writing time but also generate new writing activities and relationships that continue after retreats in micro-groups run by participants and some groups run by students.

Chapter 6 introduces a novel approach that I developed with a health professional, drawing on her work on behaviour change – the writing meeting. We developed a template that writers can use to change their writing behaviours in order to be more productive, or less stressed or to achieve their personal writing goals. This chapter describes the components of this approach: it examines the role of goal setting and monitoring for writing and explains the role of social support in achieving the behavioural changes involved in becoming a regular writer. It explains how structured discussions at these meetings prompt writers to look at their relationship with writing – often bringing ambivalence towards writing to the surface – and develop conversations and relationships with others who write.

Chapter 7 looks at the question of where these social writing activities fit in academic and professional work, since they can involve disengagement from other activities and roles. This chapter focuses on the concept of disengagement because many have argued that they *must* disengage from other tasks before they can write. It explains the forms that these disengagements take, but it also argues for a more positive interpretation: redefining disengagement from other tasks in order to write as a form of engagement with writing. It explains the role of social writing in this process.

Chapter 8 – like many other chapters in this book – borrows theory from another field. Containment theory is used to explain how these social writing activities work: by containing writing-related anxiety and making writing the primary task. It explains how social writing works and suggests why it might be working so well for those who use it.

Chapter 9 addresses the leadership role in social writing, explaining how it can be performed in a range of different ways in different settings for different groups. It explores what leadership might involve in the different forms of social writing covered in this book. It explains the research leadership role as less a process of developing people's research capacity than of helping people to recruit the capacity they already have – through social writing activities.

Chapter 10 brings together all the components identified in Chapters 1 to 9 and shows how they may be integrated in a new framework for social writing and theorises the practices of social writing. However, in order to retain a link between theorising and the experience of writing, I include vignettes of social writing. These draw on the conversations of academics, researchers and professionals about their experiences of doing social writing. These are not just my images; this is what they see and what they say.

Finally, if the idea that writing is socially constructed does not quite work for you, or if these writing theories seem too cluttered with jargon, or if they seem to lose the sense of individual agency you feel you have, or want to have, in your writing, rest assured that this book sets out a model for actively constructing your writing in your academic or professional settings, while also making it fit in with your life. And I will go easy on the jargon.

Chapter 1

Socialising writing

Writing as a social act

This chapter lays out some of the ideas I want to develop in this book, defining some of the terms I will use in this discussion. The aim is to make the concept of social writing accessible to academics, researchers, professionals and practitioners in different fields and disciplines.

Key messages

- Seeing writing as a social act means analysing the role of audiences, readers, peers, colleagues, teachers, managers and others in our writing, acknowledging their influences on our writing and understanding how we might manage or negotiate those influences.
- Making writing a social act involves writing activities that create regular planned and spontaneous interactions with some of these people.
- These conversations and relationships can be embedded in the writing process.

This book builds on a series of investigations in which I gradually became aware of the social component of writing. These studies showed how this social component – 'social' in many different senses, including social support, talking about writing, sharing plans and achievements – came to be the focus on my research and my writing.

In the first of these studies, I simply wanted to define the required skills and strategies, but I found that social support for writing was very important too. At that time I had developed a six-month writing workshop for developing skills and strategies and began to explore the extent to which people continued to use them after the workshop was over. What I discovered was that they could find no time at all for writing in their workplaces (Murray 2012a; Murray and Newton 2008).

My next study investigated what was stopping writers using strategies they knew would help them to make time for writing. I discovered that the problem, for some, was ambivalence towards scholarly writing: those who did not value journal article publication privileged other tasks and/or other types of writing, although many did not describe this as an active process. They felt they had been forced out of the scholarly writing 'game' (Murray 2007a).

I then investigated writing retreats – one way of directly addressing the need to create time for writing was by going off-campus and having dedicated time to write. I found that academics and professionals could privilege their writing at retreats, but that a retreat's impact was not always sustained, as once they returned to their workplaces they reverted to previous habits and allowed other demands to take up all their time – though that is not always how it was expressed. Again, a strong sense of lack of agency came through in interviews in this study (Murray and Cunningham 2011; Murray and Newton 2009).

The role of social writing was confirmed by a study using containment theory to explain that writing retreats work by containing writing-related anxiety, making writing the primary task and preventing anti-task behaviour (MacLeod *et al.* 2012). The leadership function in such social groupings was explored in further analysis – groups require structure and leadership and the collective, tacit or explicit agreement to work with that structure and leadership (Murray *et al.* 2012). However, it was still not clear whether they transferred these benefits to their workplaces to solve that problem.

The ongoing challenge of 'not having time to write' required a new intervention, one that could be used in academic and professional workplaces. I developed a behaviour change strategy using motivational interviewing to help writers identify discrepancies between their writing goals and their behaviours. The 'writing meeting' that I developed enabled them to align their values with external demands and provided social support as part of this process. These meetings helped writers to manage competing tasks in order to find time for writing (Murray and Thow forthcoming).

The persistent challenge of competing tasks impinging on writing was the focus of a study of 'disengagement', a component of highly productive academic writers' time management strategy (Mayrath 2008). This study showed that academics and researchers felt they had to disengage from *all* other tasks in order to engage with writing. They said that physical, cognitive and social disengagement from other tasks was needed in order to engage with writing. I created a model for engaging with writing in order to show the role played by social writing activities and relationships in creating, and protecting, dedicated writing time (Murray 2013a).

More recently I found that it is possible, after all, to transfer strategies learned at structured writing retreats to other environments, including academic and professional workplaces, by forming writing micro-groups. This study offers a solution to the 'time' problem: these micro-groups write in many timeslots and spaces, but always with people who buy into the social writing model. While writing with others is not for everyone, it can solve the problem of 'not having time to write' (Murray 2014).

Talking about writing

The common fixation on finding writing time relates to the invisibility of the act of writing. Where can we see people writing? How often do we see people writing books and articles in offices and departments? Do we hear people talking about writing? Is writing time in our workloads? Are writing-only spaces provided in our workplaces? In this context, we must construct our own writing time and space, and meeting regularly to talk about writing is part of this process.

Talking about writing can be developmental. Writers can rehearse their arguments, but they can also review their practices and construct new ones. However, I wrote this book because so many people tell me that constructing their own writing practices is not straightforward, though they know that they are supposed to find it straightforward.

I want to document the struggles that many bright, enthusiastic, hardworking people have with writing. I want to report on activities that people tell me make writing more manageable. This will include making sense of the struggles – exactly what are the difficulties? – but, more importantly, I will outline ways we have developed to make writing more enjoyable. There isn't much talk of 'joy' or 'pleasure' or even satisfaction when people start to talk about writing. Instead, there is plenty of anxiety, guilt, fear, self-censorship, anger and frustration.

Yes, they do want to 'just get on with it', but there are too many competing tasks, all laid down in workload allocations, often in specific numbers of hours. However, the act of writing is generally not included in workloads, which means that there is no allocated, dedicated writing time, and there are no deadlines for writing. This means that writing is not prioritised, since, naturally, professionally and quite rightly, we do the tasks that have deadlines before tasks without deadlines.

This book is not about diagnosing writing hang-ups. It is not about developing a therapeutic process. Nor is it about yet another way of monitoring writing. In the context of research assessment, many of us feel that collaboration, generosity and good will – so important for research – are not fostered. For many, research assessment is decimating nurturing processes. This is why social writing is so important at this time. The social writing processes that I have developed and used over the past twenty years place people on an equal footing. These social writing spaces generate good will, generosity and sharing. They initiate research dialogues and collaborations. This can be an antidote to the competitive, managerialist, capitalist discourse that purports to foster collaboration but is experienced as competition.

Developing writing relationships

As people write in groups, they begin to develop relationships around writing. They develop relatedness around writing. This sustains a new discipline and pacing for writing. This builds coherence around the act of writing. For example, the following extract from an email, from someone who was kind enough to give me feedback on the draft of a chapter, actually tracks my own evolving argument: yes, social writing practices work, but only if there is a commitment to these practices. We need to see our writing, therefore, not just as a form of active participation in a collective of one kind or another but as an expression of our commitment to writing. This means committing to the social performance of writing and experiencing the benefits that this brings to our writing, in terms of productivity and pleasure. It is not just that we 'do' social writing, but that we *are* social writers.

Why the long quotation? Because this type of material sheds light on what people do and what they think about what they do when they are trying to write. It also sheds light on the social writing model in practice, with suggestions on why and when it might work and fail.

This individual is one of those who has attended a writing group for many years, has facilitated writing groups, attended writing retreats and organised mini-retreats for colleagues. These experiences give this person a different perspective from those who have never done their writing this way, but these points are all the more valuable for that.

> There are some people in my department tasked with developing research culture . . . An opt-in informal mentoring system started, and other things. One of those things was a 'writing circle', and a colleague and I facilitated it. We set a schedule (which, instead of every Wednesday afternoon was those Wednesdays that didn't compete with the departmental research seminar series – and we made this explicit). We provided a nice snacky treat and a space (a room, the same room every time . . . [in] our building). We made sure that one or both of us was there every time. I think as many as 9 people said they would be interested in being part of this, which is why we went to the effort of putting it together.
>
> I think a total of 3 people (in addition to both of us) attended the session – a total of something like 8–10 scheduled writing sessions. One person went once, and another attended twice. That's it.
>
> We also sent out reminders the day before, so people remembered it was happening. A few people emailed early on saying they couldn't make that particular session, for whatever reason. But even that stopped midway through.
>
> My gut feeling about all of this is this: people have to commit, and they have to hold up their end. If it's impersonal – an email that goes round inviting folk – then it's too easy to abandon the plan when tired, fed up, feeling pressure from other demands or whatever.
>
> However, over that same time period, the colleague I was organising this with and I had scheduled other writing sessions in our diaries for just the two of us, and we managed to do most of those. Also, another colleague and I scheduled a couple of sessions that fit our respective diaries, and, again, we managed to do most of them – not all, mind you, but most.
>
> I think the experience of doing retreat is an important component, but also there has to be a commitment part – that by not turning up (or by cancelling), you're letting that other person down (or at least, having a less positive impact on them than if you hadn't cancelled). I think pairs or groups can informally come together and make this happen . . . But when it becomes a formal, institutional thing, it's too easy to opt out, which is why I think we had such a poor turn out. So . . . I would even emphasise the relational bit further.

Should we read this as a reminder of the potential risks of formalising social processes? Or should we interpret it as a reminder that there is no one way of writing that will suit everyone? Or should we, as suggested, 'emphasise the relational bit further'? Is it really about the importance of not only collective activity but also collective commitment? Will this relational, social model only work for some people? Will it be rejected by others/many/most? How can we know? Will fear of rejection, or fear of failing in setting up a writing group, for example, put some people off even trying to do social writing?

I think the valuable point that my colleague's email will help me to make here is that social writing is not just about the individual – there must be relationships – writing-oriented relationships – for it to work. Otherwise, we will only have the individualist model. We can understand why that individualist model is so powerful: because we are assessed as writers as individuals, and the dominant conceptualisation of writing is still that it is a solitary act, the work of an individual mind. Even in disciplines where research is done and published by groups, there will still be individualised assessments of performance.

The social writing model works both for and against this model: for, in the sense that we are writing, we are producing written outputs and we are achieving other outcomes, but also against, in the sense that we are working across disciplinary and institutional boundaries and making writing processes more overt – in our thinking and talking – than is normal in most workplaces.

Could social writing, therefore, set us apart from colleagues who write in other ways? Could we become alienated from our home discipline group? Is there a way of bridging the gap between social writing and other writing behaviours and concepts? Should social writing – in one or more of the forms described in this book – be part of research strategy? Should it be part of workload models? Should it be timetabled? Does this bring us back to the risk of formalising processes that are about relationships? Is there a fundamental tension between social writing and other activities, between writing-oriented and other workplace relationships?

Legitimising writing

If people are to solve the problem of finding time to write they need to develop the ability regularly to privilege writing over other tasks. Writing also needs to have meaning for them personally. Writers can do the work of making writing personally meaningful in social writing activities. This is not to say that academic writing requires social support, but that how academic writing is positioned creates the imperative for social support: academic writing involves competition among individuals, and writing is in competition with other tasks and roles.

There is a counter view of social writing. The following vignette of a meeting between a research leader talking to colleagues at a prestigious 'old' university, described to me by someone who was there, shows the scorn that some have for social writing:

| *Researcher:* | 'Have you ever thought of doing writing retreats?' |
| *Senior colleague:* | 'Oh no! This isn't the university of Auchtermuchty, you know . . . We can put research mentors in place, but there's not really much more we can do'. |

This research leader dismisses writing retreats as something you would only find at an obscure, tiny, low-status university. This form of social writing is represented as completely, ludicrously inappropriate for the institution where this discussion took place. The second point implies that writing is, in fact, not a social activity at all; it is up to the individual to get on with it.

Similarly dismissive is the comment of another senior officer, at another university, who responded to a colleague's research plan that included attending writing retreats:

> You don't need to go on any more of those retreats. You already have four publications for research assessment.

This comment is from the annual review of a research-active academic, who had secured significant external funding for research. This reviewer had never attended a writing retreat, but assumes that their purpose is to meet research targets, and then, it seems, there is no more need to do any more writing.

Both of these vignettes share the common misconceptions about writing retreats: that they are for those who have problems with writing rather than those who are already productive in research and writing. Such views, from such senior people, can undermine the legitimacy of retreats and of writing and will thereby prevent some people from testing it and experiencing its benefits for themselves.

There will be those who argue that social writing is only for what they probably see as the lower classes of academic or researcher or university or whatever. However, in my experience, social writing – while it is not for everyone, and while I would not want to attend a writing retreat with either of the people who made the above statements – enables those who do not write as much as they want to, to write more and helps those who already write and publish to write more and with more ease and less stress. In current workplace settings, as far as I can tell, this is an important outcome in itself.

These vignettes show how difficult it can be to legitimise writing in academic and professional settings. Even when there are activities to stimulate writing, even when there is evidence that these activities increase and/or improve outputs, some very senior people can have some very negative views of them. This is not to say that writing is impossible without senior support, but that it will be more complex where the act of writing is rendered invisible and where the assumption that people will just get on with it is asserted with such power. Nor do I want to force my argument for social writing on those who are facing the imperative for individual writing, but I would argue that legitimising writing cannot be an individual act; it is a social act, in the sense that it must take account of social settings and other people.

For those who worry that social writing will simply translate academic writing into a series of social activities, I will argue that it provides a legitimate – and legitimising – way to transform writing into a series of academic activities.

Typology of social writing

Each chapter in this book offers a different mode of social writing. Taken together, they can be represented in a typology of social writing (see Table 1.1).

All of these modes assume that we can find people to write with, perhaps in our discipline, department or workplace, or perhaps not. Perhaps we can write with people in other disciplines and spaces. Writing with others in the same discipline or line of work does not seem to matter as much as people expect it to; what seems to be more important is to write with people who buy into the social writing model and are willing to try using the *components of social writing*, which all of the above modes of social writing share:

- writing with others – communal writing;
- talking about writing-in-progress;
- discussing writing goals;
- planning and writing in real-time increments; and
- making writing the primary task.

In every chapter I try to give those who write a voice (rather than telling everyone what to do). I have had lots of conversations with writers, in my research projects and in conversations over the years, listening to what they say, thinking about

Table 1.1 Typology of social writing

Writer's Group	• On campus
	• 90 minutes, every 2 weeks
	• 5–10 people
	• Writing, giving/receiving feedback on writing or both
Writing Retreat	• Off-campus
	• 10 hours over 2 days, twice a year
	• 10–15 people
	• Writing: fixed time slots of 1 hour, 90 mins and 2 hours
Writing Meeting	• On campus
	• 2 hours, every 2 weeks, for 8 weeks
	• Pairs: 1-to-1 discussion
	• Discussing goals using Writing Meeting template
Micro-groups	• On or off-campus
	• Any time, anywhere
	• 2 or 3 people
	• Writing for 90 mins, half-day or whole day

their questions, where they agree, where they disagree, asking about what motivates them to write and what they think about the purpose of writing.

I draw on these throughout this book. In this way, you can get a sense of what happens in these discussions of writing. It is not just about having a forum for talking about writing; it is also about sharing the pleasures and satisfactions of writing. It may well be that writers' voices develop in such a forum. It is often the case that such conversations about writing cannot happen on campus and in other workplaces, where writing has no place. It is up to those who want to write to construct a place for their writing, working with others to make this a social space.

This can become a kind of collaborative work on writing processes:

- analysing diverse experiences of academic writing;
- explaining some of the most prevalent problems;
- defining and illustrating social writing strategies; and
- developing a new theory of academic writing.

It is not just that writing is a social act – which we know – but that there are social processes to mobilise the writing process – which is not so well known and not so widely practised.

'Outing' the writing process

The argument of this book is that social writing exposes writing problems and solutions, in the sense that writing in groups literally 'outs' the writing process and supports that process.

It is interesting to analyse the different components that people bring to their writing, and it is useful to think analytically about writing practices. This means talking about writing in terms of all the stages in the process – from initial idea through to outlines, drafts, multiple revisions and, finally, submission and publication – in terms of the *emerging* quality and significance of our writing, the process of constructing quality and significance and the practicalities of making time to write. This involves analysing the many components of 'making time' for writing, and social writing has an impact on people's ability to privilege writing in order to make more time for it.

These are complex issues: constructing arguments, contributing to debates, creating new knowledge and organising our time. Clearly, they are related, but there are no spaces in academic or professional settings for discussing these important issues. This is why I thought it would be useful to pull together in one book all the strategies that create these spaces and enable writers to address these issues.

Conclusion

Writing is central to academic work. We express our ideas, describe our research and construct new knowledge in writing. We progress in our careers through writing. We develop our thinking through peer review of our writing. As academics and researchers we 'act' through writing. Defining and explaining how we perform this act is itself an academic act, as we express and examine our writing practices and open them up to potential commentary from other writers in a supportive environment.

This chapter defined social writing, provided a typology of activities and introduced key components of social writing. The rationale for social writing in academic and professional settings was developed throughout this chapter.

Socialising writing means:

- writing with others (i.e. communal writing, rather than co-authoring);
- talking about writing at various stages in the process; and
- identifying people with whom you can – and cannot – have these conversations.

Social writing does not just mean talking about writing; it means using the structures and practices of social writing that are explained in the rest of this book, starting with the next chapter which focuses on developing social writing at writing groups.

Chapter 2

Becoming a writer

This chapter describes the first form of social writing I developed in the early 1990s: writer's group. This was designed to support staff who were new to higher education and, mostly, novices in research. I distinctly remember saying at the first meeting of the group responsible for coming up with a strategy to developing research capacity that a writer's group was not a 'remedial' activity. My gut feeling was that our new colleagues needed opportunities to develop relationships between themselves and their writing and between themselves and knowledge.

In the years since that first group, I developed other groups for other contexts, some of which I discuss briefly in this chapter. My aim is not simply to describe them, but to make a case for this form of relational work on writing.

Key messages

- Developing writing capacity is partly about learning new skills, partly about finding something to say – and converting that into something others might want to read – and partly about recruiting existing skills.
- Discussions of first attempts at writing can – perhaps should – address motivations and aspirations as much as topics and target journals.
- As people develop their first writing projects, regular discussions can boost their confidence and shape their writing outputs and processes.

At the first few meetings of my first writer's group I made it clear that I did not intend to teach people how to write; instead, I wanted us to engage in debate about writing, at least as a first stage. These early conversations raised questions about the place of writing in their careers and in relation to their teaching and other duties. I reasoned that if they did not have these conversations, and if any resistance to writing was taboo, or if questions about writing were ignored, they might not write at all. Furthermore, fear and anxiety about writing would probably have been even more of a barrier.

In the workplace culture which, at that time, was just beginning to develop into performativity, I felt it was important to start with people's own interests and progress from there. We did, therefore, have discussions about what this new demand – to do research and publish – was all about. Where did it come from? How would it impact on other work? Was it even feasible? While these early discussions might sound naïve now, I would argue that these are still the big questions for those writing in academic and professional settings. People are still asking these questions, and there are no one-size-fits-all answers. Nor are there opportunities to discuss these questions, and we could not assume that such discussions would be straightforward: 'Creating spaces where writers can talk about their texts is difficult given that (1) no talking space is ever neutral, and (2) . . . talking spaces are shaped by powerful institutional constraints in both teaching and research contexts' (Lillis 2009: 175).

Since then, in these increasingly performative times, Hey (2001) has urged us to resist the individualistic ethos of higher education, called for 'more collaborative ways of working' (p. 81) and – an astute point – made the case for '*persisting* in collaborative work' (Hey 2001: 40 [my emphasis]). This is another argument for relational working.

However, as long as assessment of our research and writing is individualised, the pressure is on individuals to perform (Acker and Armenti 2004: 12), whether we have – or think we have – the capacity to do so or not. In addition, this context will shape what counts as 'knowledge' and will impinge on our knowledge relations: 'This involves not simply a different evaluation of knowledge, but fundamental changes in the relationships between the learner, learning and knowledge . . . Knowledge and knowledge relations, including the relationships between learners, are de-socialized' (Ball 2003: 226).

In fact, for many of us, in many contexts, what counts as our 'work' – including our 'knowledge work' – has begun to change, and in many workplaces there is continuous change.

This was the context for setting up my first writer's groups – so that we could play an active role in the construction of knowledge and find a place for that role in our work. I had a strong sense that it was important to value the relationship that people had with their work and to define and make the case for that relationship, to see if we could make it real, personal and healthy and give it real time. They would need time to develop a relationship with this new area of work and, potentially for some, this new way of working. In fact, I hoped that writer's groups would help us counter the potentially damaging impact of the research imperative and the emphasis on solitary working.

I had, therefore, a strong feeling that writing in groups would work in some way (Elbow 1973) – I was not sure exactly what it would do, at first, but since then I have focused more and more on what we now call communities of practice (Wenger 1998). My more recent research has been about trying to explain why developing these group writing practices may be just as important as learning the technical and rhetorical skills of writing (Murray 2012a). Even more radical is my argument that writing groups may exert more positive influence on research and writing than disciplinary groups:

> A community of research practice is not solely defined by disciplinary and institutional characteristics but by commonalities in writing processes. This may be seen as challenging the conception of research and writing discourses as fixed in disciplines and departments, but what it suggests . . . is that work-places and personal lives may impact on writing as much as disciplines and that the discourse of writing practice has potential to be more inter-disciplinary than is the norm in some contexts or than is accommodated in some work-places and some processes for assessing research outputs.
>
> (Murray 2012a: 797)

Now, as I write this, decades on from my first writer's group and several years on from the study cited above, I feel I must underscore the findings of that small-scale study with the experiences of so many writers in so many disciplines and so many countries – all of whom, with a tiny percentage of exceptions, have described the benefits of writing in groups.

Thus, a writer's group could be a site for interrogating performativity, even developing a relationship with aspects of the emerging performative culture. Performativity sometimes requires the setting aside of personal values and priori-ties, and it was all too clear that we were becoming units of assessment. This is, after all, the language that is used about our writing and publications. A writer's group could, I thought, bring our values and priorities back into the conversation about our research and writing.

Starting to write in a group

This section is about how I started to get people writing in groups: it describes how I started, what worked and what failed and what I learned about writing from running writing groups. It is also about how I started to write, in the sense that writing groups helped me make writing part of my work and life.

The history of writing groups is longer than you might think (Gere 1987), particularly in the USA, and there have been many examples of creative writ-ers using this approach. More recently, they were introduced for undergraduate students to develop fluency and confidence in writing (Elbow 1973). They were then developed for postgraduates (Aitchison 2009; Aitchison and Guerin 2014) and for academic and professional staff (Botshon and Raimon 2009; Elbow and Sorcinelli 2006; Haines *et al.* 1997; Lee and Boud 2003; Murray 2008a, 2013b; Murray and Moore 2006).

When I set up my first writer's group in 1993, however, the idea of writing in a group made immediate sense to some but still sounded a bit too 'remedial' to others. The aim of my first writer's group was to help people who worked in a former college of education that had just merged with the university where I worked to start doing research and writing for publication (Murray and MacKay 1998a, 1998b). I assumed that it would be helpful to offer support for those making the transition from practitioner to researcher roles – many were former teachers involved in teacher education. I also assumed I would not know exactly what they needed or wanted by way of support in this transition – and beyond – which meant that we needed time and space to discuss what they wanted and how I thought I could help them.

We could have called this identity work (Åkerlind 2005), or research training or writing development, but it was likely to be a combination of all three – and possibly more – and meeting in a writer's group had the advantage of not disguising what we were setting out to do in concepts that we would probably all define differently. It also held our focus on writing.

Participants in that first group were a mixture: people who wanted to do research but did not know how, people who were already registered for higher degrees or wanted to start one and those who were already doing some research, in an almost covert way. A few people turned up to see what was happening, to challenge the drivers for research or to tell us that they had no time to do research because they were too busy doing teaching and administration. Almost all of those who came to the first meeting and stayed in the group for the next two years were committed to engaging in research.

The format of this writer's group was developed around participants' needs and availability (see Appendix A for guidelines on setting up writing groups).

Format of the first writer's group:

- regular meetings
- for two hours
- twice a month
- including writing time
- setting goals for short, medium and long term
- discussing writing-in-progress
- giving and receiving feedback on practices and texts
- supportive relationships
- self-selecting participants

Although finding times to suit everyone was time-consuming in itself, we thought it was important in order to ensure that those who wanted to participate could do so. I acted as facilitator at these meetings, providing guidance on academic writing, while the faculty research coordinator shared knowledge of potential target journals in the field and insights into participants' work settings. We spent time at each meeting on strategies for getting started in writing and developing and revising journal articles. There was also time to discuss participants' issues: finding time to write, barriers to writing, developing ideas into articles and the balance of writing and other tasks.

Running that group gave me, the other facilitator and the participants insights into the process of transitioning into being a writer. We learned that there are probably key moments in that process, and these moments occurred in our earlier conversations rather than in writing meetings, which came later:

- Discussing personal interests – what do you want to find out?
- Expressing opinions and polemic – what do you want to say?
- Thinking about how to do research – does anything stand in your way?
- What are your views on external drivers – research assessment?
- Who or what will help or inhibit your research and writing?

These questions were not on our agenda – in any sense – when I set up this group, but they became the obvious starting point for future groups: if people did not have a chance to discuss these questions, it was unlikely that they would find ways to engage in research and writing – that was my thinking. Would these issues have been raised in other settings? To the same extent? It seems unlikely that they would have been discussed in exactly the same terms, but these are useful pointers.

One participant's writing illustrates the persistent concerns of people in this first group, at this early stage in a research career and in the early stages of a writing project:

> by the end of the [writer's group] meeting, I had thought of so many things that I need to do that I began to panic about when to do them all . . . I was a bit envious when most of the others spoke of how they intended to set aside some time during the working day. That, unfortunately, is a bit of a luxury as far as I am concerned.
>
> (Murray 2002: 232)

> At the very early stages of the writing process, the step between an idea for a paper and the actual publication is enormous. However, as the topic and themes are developed, target dates are set and initial drafts are subjected to peer review, the enormous step is transformed into a series of more gradual steps, interspersed with landings or stages for review and reflection. The whole process becomes more manageable.
>
> (Murray 2002: 233–234)

Our conversations showed that participants did have knowledge and skills they could use for writing journal articles, but that some recognised that this was a different genre, about which they still had much to learn. We realised that writing need not be a solitary activity, and that writing in groups not only provided support but also helped us develop our ideas. We also noted we did not have what we could call dedicated time for writing, even though writing required dedicated time. This prompted our next move: to include writing time in our group meetings. This experience of writing in the group immediately created dedicated writing time.

Throughout the lifetime of that group we shared writing goals. We developed insight into each other's research – in an education faculty there is a wide range of approaches, on the quantitative-to-qualitative spectrum. These exchanges would not have happened during normal working time.

It seems simplistic to say that meeting to talk about our research and meeting to write will grow our relationship to knowledge, will build relationships between researchers and will develop participants' relationships to their knowledge and their writing. Moreover, it seems obvious that relational writing will grow relationships. However, this very simple process does seem to facilitate these quite complex processes. The simplicity of the model should not, therefore, blind us to developments in these relationships – not just relationships with others who write, but relationships between us and the components of writing, including time, space and other people. The trick is to find enough likeminded people, and perhaps, at first, a facilitator, to make it happen.

This is not, of course, the only way to do writer's group. In addition to the fixed form of my first group, there are more formalised and fluid forms (see Table 2.1).

The 'fixed' type is illustrated by my first writer's group. The 'formalised' type is exemplified by a departmental group I ran for one department, meeting every two weeks for several years, which was endorsed by the department, with the Head of Department attending – i.e. writing at – almost every meeting. The more recent 'fluid' groups have formed out of writing retreats, an important development – students and researchers running groups for themselves – described in the section on micro-groups in Chapter 5.

These lists show differences between the three and illustrate how diverse writer's groups can be in form and function. For example, while my early groups were 'fixed' in the sense that they focused on the needs of one group, always met in the same place and with the same people, one post-retreat micro-group has a floating membership of forty, who do not attend all meetings, which are held in many different places, depending on availability, and are run by participants. In fact, members of this larger 'fluid' group meet in multiple sub-groups in potentially different groupings at every meeting.

Since I started my first writer's group, there have been many developments in this area. There has been work on developing a pedagogy for postgraduate groups

Table 2.1 Forms of writing group

Fixed	Formalised	Fluid
Same participants	Mostly the same people	Different every time
Self-selecting/directed	Self-selecting/advised	Self-selecting
Attending all meetings	At most meetings	When available
Faculty strategy	Endorsed by department	Personal commitment
Similar experience	Range of experiences	New researchers
Novice	More experienced	Research active
Meeting outside department	In department	Anywhere
Timed to suit participants	Same timeslot	Any timeslot/duration

(Aitchison 2009; Aitchison and Lee 2006; Aitchison *et al.* 2010), and there has been research on how academics and professionals deploy these practices (Lee and Boud 2003; Murray 2012a). This strengthens the argument for writer's group not only as a way of developing novices' research capacity but also of supporting the research activity of experienced researchers and, perhaps – using different forms of writer's group, as required and as available – throughout the research career lifecycle.

'Writers' and 'non-writers'

> Lots of people have great ideas, but few finish the race.

This statement from a novice writer – new to higher education but having attended regular writer's group meetings over a period of years – conveys, I think, his sense of the gap between his 'idea' and a potential publication. This hits the nail on the head. He recognised that people have the potential to research and write, but can be inhibited by any number of factors during the lengthy process of writing an article.

This is why it was so important to focus on practice – to talk about writing as a practice. This meant 'outing' the various stages and many hurdles and, to some extent, as far as possible, normalising them. This provided opportunities to change writing practices. For some, writer's group was the difference between writing and not writing, between publishing and not publishing:

> The very first paper I got published in a journal article was one that I had worked at over the writer's group meetings and [the facilitator] gave me feedback on. It was finally published in 1997, so that wouldn't have happened without the writer's group at all. And that particular piece has actually been cited . . . quite a few times, and I wouldn't have done that had the writer's group not sort of said, choose something, work at it, and I will give you feedback . . . I wouldn't have got where I've got to without that little push and support.

However, others did not find a place for writing in their professional time; instead, it ate into their personal time:

> When I went to the first [writer's group] 10 years ago I did manage to follow some of [the facilitator's] strategies, like trying to write for 10 minutes each day, like snacking, but that was mainly whilst I was actually on her writer's group. But . . . I'm doing the binge writing, where you suddenly get a batch of time and really, really work at that solidly. Well solidly would mean coming in here and keeping completely away from everything at the weekend and just writing the whole of the weekend and trying to actually get something done, because I don't have any time, like, for example, there is no day in semester 2 that I'm not teaching. My teaching load is very heavy, so it tends to be summer time, Easter holiday time, weekend time and you can then blast something out. So trying to actually map out protected times have often gone by the wayside.

More than ten years later, I followed up people in that first writer's group to find out whether or not they were still writing and publishing, continued to use the strategies we developed then and were still writing in groups and/or in other ways.

By doing this I wanted to stimulate reflection and action, but also to shed light on the perceived culture for writing and changes that had occurred in writers' perceptions of that culture between 1994, when the first writer's group was formed, and 2007, when I secured funding from Strathclyde University for this study.

Ten of the academics who had attended the first writer's group participated in this study, which was almost all of that first group. There were two other people whom we could not track down. We did three one-hour individual interviews with each of the ten participants. The aims of the study were:

- to explore with participants their memories of participating in writer's group;
- to discuss their current writing goals, practices and aspirations; and
- to establish the impact of writer's group on their writing practice and published output.

My intention was not to evaluate either these writers' outputs or the long-term impact of the writer's group they attended. Instead, I wanted to find out what they wanted to say about writing, what was on their agendas, not mine.

In order to uncover participants' perspectives, the first interview began with a general prompt: I asked them if they remembered anything about the writer's group at all and, if so, what. The discussions then progressed in a number of different directions, with me sharing my views and experiences, so that it was more like a dialogue than an interview. These first interviews were not recorded. I took notes during the discussions and then summarised my notes at the end of the interviews, when I identified a theme in our discussion and asked interviewees to comment on that. This step let me check my summary with participants, and often led to further discussion.

Two further interviews were conducted by a researcher employed for this project. The themes emerging from these interviews were that the writer's group prompted them to get started, demystified the writing process and taught them about the genre of writing for publication.

The following responses shed light on the perceived culture for writing:

Can you describe the culture for writing for publication in your working environment?

The culture of publication is that the university wants us to be researchers and to be published researchers, such that our output would be sufficient to count towards the RAE [UK Research Assessment Exercise], and it raises the standard of staff in line with our peers by having publications and has the consequence of raising the standing of the university within the academic field.

What sort of things do they do to enable you to do this?

Nothing.

So there are no systems that you can tap into that would enable you to do research?

Other than something like the writer's group, which is just going to encourage you to write . . . there is nothing you can tap into on a regular basis that would give encouragement and support.

On strategies they learned then and were still using ten years later, they included 'snacking', 'just writing', goal setting, developing the writing habit, structure, shared writing, developing networks and targeting journals.

In terms of publications, this group appeared to have split right down the middle: five had regularly produced scholarly publications and five had been writing for other purposes and audiences. I am uncomfortable distinguishing these two sets of writers in the following terms, because I do not want to contribute to the construction of two tribes – writers and non-writers – but five of them *self-identified* as non-writers, so I will use that term here.

'Writers'

- Reported that there was support for writing, though lack of a culture of research in the department.
- Displayed a high level of intrinsic motivation to write.
- Felt that personal qualities helped them to write: thick skin, determination, passion for the subject, desire to communicate, curiosity, seeking new insight and challenges.

'Non-writers'

- Reported that there was no support for research and writing.
- Did not want to write.
- Identified factors that hindered their writing: anxiety and prioritising other professional tasks.
- Saw writing as a distraction from the 'real work' of teaching.

Some of the most productive were those who had developed relationships around writing:

So you're part of a sort of network of writers?

I'm part of lots of networks, different pieces of work I show to different people depending on their interest and expertise. One piece I've just had published I showed to a friend who is in the [government department]. She is not an academic, but she's at the heart of government. It was on policy making, and I was very grateful for her comments on how she saw the work. So I use all sorts of people. I use my wife quite a lot, who reads my work. Although she is not an expert in the field she makes lots of good stylistic comments on just how readable it is. Even before I came to the writer's group I showed stuff to . . . my wife and she frequently points out clumsy or inelegant sentences. I think showing your work to other people is critically important if you want quality and readability.

This illustrates what developing relationships between writing, work and life might mean and shows how these relationships may be conceptualised as part of the writing process.

The following quotes from interviews illustrate these writers' intrinsic motivation, but they also show many of the relational components of writing: the urge to communicate with others in the 'public domain', the link between writing and people's values, intersections of different values, the role of others in the development of writers' self-esteem, relationships between writing and other tasks and roles, the relationship between different types of writing and the emotions each triggers, relationships with research mentors, explaining the relationship between the drafting process and the final product, relating writing to real time and the relationship between the individual and his or her environment. There is also the more negative, or positive, depending on one's perspective, 'relationship' of nepotism:

> I said to myself: the only way that you're going to continue to have a rewarding job in here is by reflecting on your experience and practice and putting it out into the public domain where people can comment, give you feedback.

> The professor has tried to link it to strengths of people, linking it to what they value, trying to get what's valued in one field valued in another. The hierarchies are there with other issues – who people rate and don't – it's not just about writing. It even comes down to courses – teaching on certain courses has more status than teaching on other courses. It's just nonsense, but it's there. It's been a cause of tension in the department – even down to 'what is an hour?': is sitting writing and thinking for one hour not as hard as one hour of teaching? This is an external factor that's forcing people to value one thing more than another, when we all know it's not straightforward. It's forcing folk to take sides.

> There's a dirtiness to the whole thing – having a brass neck and getting on to editorial boards and writing chapters for a book and then you get funding – It's about who knows who. People write and publish with their cronies. This affects my motivation to write. To be in the 'in crowd' . . . you've got to have the self-esteem that maintains the motivation. Who might I feel that I could bare my soul with? I'm making it too personal – too self-interested in writing.

I recognise I need to do a different type of writing . . . for my own personal satisfaction . . . although I recognise that it's not considered worthy because it's not RAE-rated [UK Research Assessment Exercise]. I recognise a need to do a different kind of writing . . . for my own personal satisfaction, and because I know the university rates that kind of writing more . . . In some senses it angers me.

Partly as result of writer's group and conversations with [facilitators], made me put a 5-year plan together. I got to year 3 and was then scuppered. I got delayed by other work. Had projects to tender for – it was a golden opportunity. This will lead to publications. . . . I need people commenting on and responding to my writing. I've got a good mentor to do that.

[Writer's group] was a turning point, in terms of confidence. It's no use giving your writing to someone who's just going to say it's fine. Before, I would never have gone to someone and asked them to tear it to bits. Now I do. I do 8 to 15 drafts now – a lot of which are major rewrites.

I do remember something: writing in small chunks. That's a very important idea. Writing in huge amounts of time only – it's a myth. Subdividing the work into small sections. 30 minutes or an hour – concentrated. You can actually move the thing forward. It will need more work, but you feel good. It's extremely influential.

It's not just up to the individual, though it comes back to individual disposition.

The point of listing all of these relational aspects is to raise the question about the extent to which they may be addressed – and potentially developed – in a writer's group. These comments suggest that they play an important role. In fact, we can see that writing is made up of many relational aspects. This is not to say that those who do not write are to be cast out. They may not have had the experiences that might have led them to develop perseverance. They may have had destructive experiences, as had one of the participants in this study:

I was invited to chair a research seminar . . . Ended up in a very aggressive group. Everything I was saying was very threatening to what they stood for. That really shook me. It really shook my confidence. Particularly one person who pursued me, sending me articles as if I knew nothing. . . . You can experience some very damaging events. I just closed down. I cut off a lot of academic and research networks across the country. I refused to write a paper for a conference. I shut it all down.

This is a classic anti-relational experience, with a completely anti-relational response and outcome. This person cut off all relations with others in the network and ended the relationship with writing itself: 'I shut it all down'. We do not really know whether this experience is widespread or exceptional. All we can say is that it made this writer value writing less:

> I began to get very cynical – was anything worth researching at all? We should be getting on with our job rather than contemplating our navels. I was reading [published] papers and thinking, 'So?'

This sobering insight into the pressures on people in relation to writing is an important reminder of differences not only in writers' personal attributes but also in their experiences. For me, it only strengthens the case for building relationships around writing that would support someone who has this experience. We all have our writing rejected at some point, perhaps not so destructively as in this example, but perhaps it would not have been so destructive if this person had discussed the experience in a writer's group? A writer's group is not just a support group for novice writers or therapy for rejected writers; it can help writers negotiate potentially – and actually – destructive relationships in/with their writing.

Developing relational capacity

The ability to develop relational capacity and competence requires certain strengths: empathy, openness to vulnerability, the capacity to experience and express emotion, the ability to participate in another person's development, the expectation that relational interactions will be opportunities for learning and development for all parties involved (Marshall *et al*. 2011: 67).

Where can we develop this capacity and competence? Where are we able safely to be open to vulnerability? Do we feel empathy towards our colleagues, and do we expect empathy from them?

What happens when there is no relationship? Or where there is a disconnect between, say, writing and life? Writing and eating? Writing and friendship or partner? Writing and colleagues at work?

Where can we express emotion at work? In relation to our writing? Is that even appropriate? Can we not have emotions related to writing, and can/do we not express them in some way?

What does 'participate in another person's development' mean? Are we all to become staff developers? Is somebody else ignoring their mentoring responsibilities here? Or is this discourse inappropriate? 'But to recognise and name such attributes means bringing the language and meaning of the private/home sphere into the workplace' (Marshall *et al*. 2011: 67) – some would see that as a 'violation', or even an attempt to instil vulnerability by crossing the boundary between private and public life. If so, the result is that we cannot use that vocabulary and those concepts to discuss our work. This may be how the act of writing is made to disappear: we cannot talk about the process, about our emotions, vulnerabilities and uncertainties that are involved in developing new knowledge in and through writing.

What is the 'strong, valued language' (Marshall *et al.* 2011: 67) that we might use to talk about relational writing? Does strong language for talking about relational writing include the words I chose for titles of my chapters? – rhetoric, skill, structure, engagement, containment, leadership, productivity. On the other hand, what would constitute 'weak' language for talking about relational writing? – cooperation, collegiality, connectedness, emotion, vulnerability, trust, empathy, mutuality? These are the ideas I seek to develop in the sections of my chapters. The so-called strong words are those we more regularly use in talking about our writing; the so-called weak words are not so familiar in this context.

What I am trying to do in this book is to develop a relationship between the two. I do not want to kick the so-called strong words into touch, but to reconfigure them in relational terms. The result will still be productivity – to use one of the strong words that has most currency in workplace discussions of writing – but it will be relational. In fact, relationality is, for many, directly associated with their productivity in writing. In the same vein, structure and containment will sound strong, mechanistic and even controlling to some, but they provide the mechanisms for developing relationships in and through writing. These ideas and practices support relationality; they don't control it.

All the forms of social writing described in this chapter are about integrating life and work, making connections between the two, bridging the gap between them. Social writing activities allow writers to imagine and enact possibilities for writing in different settings and circumstances. It also grows relationships between the disciplines.

Spretnak (2011) talks about Relational Shift: moving away from anti-relational ways of knowing and being towards a relational way of seeing not just writing but the planet – relationality as world view. This suggests that we can think about relationality in terms of not only relationships between people, but also relationships between writing and other activities, and food, space, furniture, clothing, music, time and other work roles and tasks – this book explores the idea of developing those relationships and considers some ways of doing that, like a writer's group.

Conclusion

When I first started running writer's groups it quickly became clear that they were having a positive impact on participants' confidence and productivity, especially for people who were new to writing, but also for me. For some people, this was the first conversation they had ever had about their writing. Even sceptics, once they tried this approach, found it was useful, although, of course, there were always those who would not even try it.

The purpose of the first few groups I ran was not only to boost productivity; it was also to create environments where people, including myself, could negotiate the many tensions and difficulties of academic writing. A writer's group meeting was a space where we could interrogate assumptions and negotiate organisational demands. We began to form communities of writers and/or research communities (Lave and Wenger 1991; Murray 2012a):

- negotiating barriers to writing
- carving out routes to writing
- seeking out support for writing
- finding multiple forms of participation in writing
- negotiating latent sense of exclusion from writing
- negotiating competing values – own and others'
- managing pressure, power and control
- growing meaning and value in/of writing.

Writer's groups might be particularly valuable in settings where large numbers of people are starting to do research and write – such as new universities or research centres, for example – and where the aim is to boost research activity – which could be practically anywhere.

The components of social writing involved in writing groups are:

- talking about writing with others who want to write – talking about ideas, motivations, views, values, experiences and purposes;
- learning about their work, talking about yours; and
- talking about writing processes, contents and practices, exposing the specifics of writing to comment, reflection and critique.

Once people have developed relational skills, some feel they have 'outgrown' a 'fixed' group, which is not to say that they, as writers, have been 'fixed' or become 'fixed', but that they have other needs and are want to develop other relationships:

> For a lot of people, talking about writing was the same as doing it. They see writing as very difficult, with competing demands, which is true, but the task is just do it – I did not find it interesting to listen to problems and reasons and excuses. There was quite a lot of that. They 'talked the talk', but what were their outputs then? In what period of time? I felt I'd outgrown that particular group of people – got impatient.

Is this about outgrowing a specific group? Will a writer's group only take new writers so far? Does this comment signal a need for other relationships? Does this suggest a need for other skills? This writer's group had, after all, an explicit introductory function – to initiate research activity through writing. What do we do when some participants choose not to move on? What do we do when different motivations emerge in the group? How do we extend the developments that occur in writer's groups?

The next step could be to engage in formal study of research methods, of research management and of academic writing itself. The idea of a formal course on academic writing was radical at the time, but that is exactly what I did next. Its aim was not just to meet the needs of people who had 'outgrown' their writer's groups, since groups continued to run and were still valued; instead, it was to support those who had started writing and realised they needed or wanted to learn more about it. I admit that, in some instances, their views might have been shaped by my regular references to the vast literature on academic writing.

The next chapter describes the formal, credit-bearing course on academic writing that I developed. It discusses participants' responses to this course and explains how it seemed to meet a real need among academics and professionals, even those who were already writing, publishing and using writing in their teaching. This course also created relationships between writing in teaching and research roles (Murray 2001).

Chapter 3

Becoming rhetorical

Becoming 'rhetorical' means recognising the importance of shaping writing for specific audiences and choosing an appropriate purpose for our writing for a specific audience. This involves knowing what that means in terms of how we construct the text. It involves recognising that this may be a learning process. As with all the chapters in this book, I argue that social writing can facilitate this learning and these rhetorical practices.

Putting the rhetorical principle into practice can be complex. It involves audience analysis – assessing an audience's requirements and expectations, which are not always overt and clear. It means exploring relationships between the 'message' we want to convey in our writing and the current discourse, including others' writing on the subject. As I argued in a previous chapter, these negotiations with writing – one's own and others' – can be performed, supported and enhanced by social writing in groups. In this chapter I will explain that these negotiations can include the nature and structure of argument.

The word 'rhetorical' is often used to mean the opposite of clarity and open attempts at persuasion; it is often used in a reductive sense, when something is said to be *merely* rhetorical – i.e. lacking substance or credibility – while the word 'rhetoric' is often used to define what is considered to be empty writing or speech, which is the very opposite of persuasive.

For the purposes of this chapter rhetoric is not about manipulating people, but it is about using writing to influence people. We aspire to using our knowledge to change things for the better. In many different senses, in many different disciplines, we are all doing research because we want to add to knowledge. In order to do that we need to write persuasive texts. We have to persuade our audience – sometimes a range of audiences – that we have something new, useful or worthwhile, sometimes in different senses, to say. We have to get them to see that our work has value. We must persuade them that our writing is worth reading – and that they can see the value of our work in our writing. We must, therefore, use persuasive writing techniques. This is what I mean by rhetoric: the skills of writing persuasive argument.

In this chapter the word 'rhetoric' appears alongside the word 'composition' because I draw on my experience of teaching the subject Rhetoric and

Composition in the USA when I was doing a PhD in English at the Pennsylvania State University. In that context, rhetoric referred to persuasive argument while composition referred to expository, or descriptive, writing. However, there is a view that all forms of writing are rhetorical in the sense that all writing is intended for a specific audience and a specific purpose.

Becoming rhetorical is, I think, a key stage in the academic writer's development: the point at which we shift from a primary focus on what we want to say to realising the importance of what others want to hear. This realisation often prompts an adjustment in thinking and writing: from asserting a point to arguing it. I often see this in PhD students' writing and speech, when they realise that they have to adjust what they write about their research for specific audiences (Murray 2010a). For example, they often start by overstating their critique of policy, theory or literature and later realise that a more balanced account, identifying pros and cons, is more precise. This is a negotiation – it is not a sudden change of perception but an inherent requirement of writing and thinking. My point is that writing always involves such negotiations. Managing them is part of writing.

For some, initially and/or in some disciplines, this will seem ridiculous – if our research has merit and value it will be published; if it hasn't, it won't. It is as simple as that. For others, to talk about writing as 'negotiation' is to spell out the blindingly obvious – of course we have to adapt our writing to a specific audience. Others consider that by writing they enter a debate and therefore need to take into account many different views as they offer their own views in writing.

Key messages

- 'Becoming rhetorical' does not mean learning how to manipulate people; it means focusing on audience and purpose for writing.
- We can use the literature on rhetoric and composition to learn about structures and styles for constructing our texts.
- Developing our writing can involve both formal and informal learning: formal learning in a credit-bearing course and informal learning through group writing activities during and after such a course.
- Social writing is a way of developing rhetorical skills, and rhetoric provides a range of topics for discussion in social writing settings.

The purpose of putting the subject of rhetoric here, at this point in the book, is not to prop up the modes of informal learning described in previous chapters with the idea of a formal course; instead, my aim is to show how formal courses can incorporate social writing activities.

I am not going to compare and contrast formal and informal learning, but argue that they both have a role. This argument needs to be made strongly at this time because, I think, there is a lack of awareness at best, and open hostility at worst, to the very idea of academics – or even students – having 'tuition' in writing. However, not learning about academic writing is likely to mean that writing – and consequently, thinking, reading and research – may be more onerous, stressful and time-consuming than it needs to be, even for bright people.

I should say at this point that I myself had never attended or even heard of a course on academic writing before I was required to teach Rhetoric and Composition, but I know that there is demand for what we might now call writing development or support, particularly in the current context of pressures to publish.

This is not to say that I think everyone should take a course on academic writing. There are not enough courses. It is simply not feasible. Nor am I saying that we should all become writing teachers, although there are topics in this chapter that can be used to support undergraduate and postgraduate students' writing (Eley and Murray 2009; Lee and Murray forthcoming).

I should also own up to the origins of my views – in the many years of supporting academics, researchers and students who struggle with writing. For many years it was my job to help them. For many years I helped people at a number of universities, in different disciplines and in different higher education cultures, in the UK and overseas. Although that is no longer my job, I continue to help people in that way, and I think I have enough contact with people who write in many different academic and professional settings to know that the problem has not gone away. I hope I am not overstating my role here – I am merely anticipating valid questions about how I know that there is any need, interest or demand for formal instruction in academic writing before, during and beyond the doctorate.

It is difficult to know the scale of this problem – that is true. It is difficult to define the role of 'writing' in, for example, late PhD submissions or non-submissions, rejected articles or conference papers that were never written up for journals. It is difficult to account for the relative absence of practitioners' views in research debates. However, surely we can agree that writing is likely to be implicated, to some extent, in these problems? Perhaps we can agree that it is, at least, worth thinking about whether or not rhetorical development might impact on them?

When I propose that a solution to the problem might lie in formal learning about writing, specifically in terms of rhetoric and composition, I admit that my thinking has been shaped by my experience of teaching writing during my PhD in the USA. Although I wrote well and did well in my undergraduate studies, it was not until I learned about rhetoric and composition that I began to take control of my writing – in the sense of focusing my reading, thinking, talking and structuring my texts. I began to manage the writing process better, taking time to think and develop my ideas, rather than getting them down in a mad rush and handing my papers in at the last minute. This also dramatically raised the standard of my writing – and thinking – and reduced the stress of writing.

In the next two sections I draw on my experience of, first, teaching Rhetoric and Composition in a US university and, second, developing a module on

Academic Writing in a UK university. They therefore move from the US to the UK, from the role of writing teacher to academic developer and from undergraduate to academics' writing.

These sections provide insights into the experiences of academics who were students on the UK module, and anonymised emails and extracts from conversations show how important social writing practices were for their development as writers. In addition, they show how those who took this course began to use social writing in their teaching.

Learning to write

> Successful lecturers are likely to have spent many years developing acceptable ways of constructing their own knowledge through their own writing practices in a variety of disciplinary contexts.
>
> (Lea and Street 1998: 163)

In one sense, I agree with this statement: I agree that lecturers are likely to have had extensive experience of writing in different settings and for different purposes during their undergraduate and postgraduate courses and thereafter. However, I disagree with the idea that their experience will have helped them all to develop ways of constructing texts. It might have, but not for everyone. I also disagree with the implication – perhaps unintended, perhaps just my interpretation – that this is where learning about writing stops, that these 'many years' of learning are likely to be sufficient. I know that's not true. I also wonder about whether this statement means that only those who are 'successful' will have – or be seen to have – the required knowledge and skills in writing. What about the rest? What about those who are not yet 'successful'?

This raises another question about those with a teaching role: has their experience of constructing their knowledge through writing prepared them – all of them? – to include writing in their teaching? Do they pass on their knowledge about writing to undergraduate and postgraduate students? Do similarly experienced professionals pass on their knowledge to emerging researchers in their fields? Do they all teach others to construct their knowledge in writing, as they themselves have done, and/or do they offer alternatives to how they did it? Do they all have the capacity, time and inclination to do that?

Most lecturers I've met are quite clear that they do not see themselves as teachers of writing. They do not see their role as involving passing on their knowledge about writing to students. Many are adamant that there should be some instruction in writing, as students move through different stages of a degree and are required to produce different forms and levels of writing. Many have strong views on the standard of student writing, and some are critical of the standard or value of published writing in their fields. Usually, they are unaware of the literature on academic writing, or of Writing to Learn or Writing Across the Curriculum – to name but two established seams of inquiry in the field of academic writing.

Then there is the other view:

> I find it rather astonishing that such tuition is required – how did these staff get good first degrees and then higher degrees? If any further help is required in shaping an article, does not the head of department provide this for junior staff?
> (Anonymous reviewer of an article I submitted
> to a UK education journal)

So, there are people who think that there is no need for 'tuition' in writing, once you have completed your degrees, and who will not hesitate to say so. This can be off-putting for novice researchers, who may already be unclear about – not so much how to write, but about how to produce the kinds of texts that meet the standards of examiners and peer reviewers who may think the same way as the reviewer quoted above.

This is not an attempt to get back at this reviewer, but to open up for discussion an assumption about how writing gets done and how we learn(ed) to do it. I do not think we can know how widely held, or otherwise, this reviewer's opinion is, but we do know that some people think this. In discussing this review, others have read into it an elitism, a wielding of power that personalises the critique of the writer rather than the writing.

Or is this reviewer, by suggesting that the solution to writing problems lies in discussion between senior and junior staff, actually advocating social writing? Perhaps not, since the reference to 'tuition' suggests that the problem lies in lack of writing skills, rather than a lack of social writing practices?

Another take on this question is provided by academics and professionals who are new to higher education, and/or working in disciplines that are new to higher education, where research is still developing. They sometimes have high levels of expertise and extensive experience in their areas, but have little or no research training or experience. This means that there is perhaps more variety in higher education and professional fields than the review quoted above suggests. This diverse population of emerging researchers may have recently completed a higher degree, may have started to publish, and they *are* likely to benefit from 'tuition' in writing, which is another reason for writing a chapter on this topic.

The subject of how we learn to do academic writing is awash with assumptions and myths. Perhaps both of those views miss the mark. No, it cannot be assumed that everyone who writes a thesis or journal article or completes two degrees will have spent years developing ways of constructing knowledge through their writing practices, and, no, we cannot say that tuition is not required. For me, these two views are at opposite ends of the spectrum. My course on academic writing is probably somewhere near the midpoint of that spectrum.

The value of such a course then, when I invented it, and even more so now, is that there is a vast literature on academic writing, including practical strategies, theoretical positions, empirical work, case studies, evaluations, narratives and accounts of writers' development. This work is located in and/or draws on many disciplines – literacy, rhetoric, linguistics, psychology, education, health, neurology, sociology. Some of it crosses disciplinary boundaries. It is a body of work that has produced practical strategies for writing in many disciplines.

I have reviewed some of the literature on academic writing elsewhere (Murray 2011b: 22–24). The main developments in the field are a shift from technical skills to social processes and the long-overdue synergy between research on writing conducted in the USA and elsewhere in the world. There is still plenty of guidance on writing practices, but much more scrutiny of how such practices are constructed and shaped. A focal point has been on writing development for postgraduate research students, where, it has been argued, most of the literature focuses on the 'appropriation of disciplinary discourse conventions' (Rose and McClafferty 2001: 27). Others argue that academic writing should create new conventions, new genres and include new voices (Kamler and Thomson 2008: 513).

Whatever we think research students should learn about writing, Caffarella and Barnett's (2000) findings remind us that students may find giving and receiving feedback to be the most useful way of developing their writing – it's not all on us! This underscores the social and relational model of writing, so it would be useful if students had opportunities to experience these practices and to discuss their views on them.

While 'how to' books on thesis writing have been criticised (Kamler and Thomson 2008), I would argue that most research supervisors should know at least some of these books on academic writing and check that their students know about some of them too (Eley and Murray 2009). Even if there are no discipline-specific writing texts – and in some areas there are none – some of these books can help students work out how to take their writing to the next level for a conference abstract, journal article, thesis chapter, transfer document or progress report.

To sum up, on the subject of learning about writing, there are plenty of textbooks, there is empirical research and there are theoretical frameworks and practical strategies. However, while the rest of this chapter focuses on writing courses, these courses include relational activities. For example, components of writer's groups – covered in the previous chapter – were introduced into workshops and seminars, thus incorporating relational activities in 'learning to write'.

Rhetoric and composition

If you had been an undergraduate at an American university, you are likely to have studied Rhetoric and Composition. You might have done two compulsory courses during your undergraduate years, written seven to ten papers in each course and learned some rhetorical principles. As part of these courses you would probably have read and analysed examples of rhetorical principles in some of the best fiction, non-fiction and journalism of the day.

To take but one example of a Rhetoric and Composition course, there is the Pennsylvania State University, when I was a PhD student there, which was not yesterday, but it will suffice to illustrate my point. I apologise to those who work in this area if what follows seems like a gross simplification of a great course. For a more detailed account, see Fahnestock and Secor (1990). My aim is not to simplify, but to show the value of courses on Rhetoric and Composition that cover skills of writing exposition and argument, not only for undergraduates but also for postgraduates and researchers.

The course on expository writing covered seven rhetorical modes, and students wrote a paper on each of them: description; narration; process; analysis; compare and contrast; classification; and definition, which combined all the modes of exposition. The course on argument covered five modes: categorical proposition, causal analysis, evaluation, refutation and proposal, which combined all the modes of argument. (See Appendix B for Rhetoric and Composition: Modes of Writing.)

Every undergraduate student took these two courses. Multiply the number of students at the Pennsylvania State University by the number of universities where these courses are taught, consider the number of textbooks this requires and the amount of research and scholarship it generates, and you will get a sense of the scale – and range and depth – of the field known as Rhetoric and Composition.

In order to teach this course, I had to take three postgraduate modules, including teaching strategies and activities and, crucially for me, since I had never even heard of such a course before I went to study in the USA, guidance on assessment. My teaching was observed by staff in the Composition Unit (of the English department) who were appointed mentors to new tutors. Every semester I had student evaluations of my teaching, in which I had to achieve a specific standard, or I would not be allowed to teach the course and could lose the Graduate Assistantship that paid my PhD fees and my stipend.

Teaching this course involved explaining and discussing each of the rhetorical modes, using the course textbook, illustrating it with examples from the course reader and helping students to develop their ideas, outlines and drafts of their papers. I taught three classes a week in a ten-week semester and marked thirty-plus papers for each assignment. (Did I mention that I was also doing a PhD?)

Teaching this course had a profound impact on me. At first, I found it completely alien. When I read my first set of students' papers, I thought I would have to fail them all. I could not see how their writing – either in technical terms or in terms of content, which included a lot of opinion and personal narrative – could count towards a grade. Thankfully, with good mentoring and instruction I was able to adjust my criteria to suit this course. Gradually, I realised that students were learning how to organise their ideas and their writing by learning about these rhetorical modes.

Gradually, my own writing began to benefit. I began to see that there were specific purposes for each mode and specific uses to which you could put them in academic writing – not just for these undergraduate assignments but also for my PhD writing. For example, I used classification for a literature review, organising all the literature around an issue, and grouping the literature according to what selected authors had said about that issue. For another literature review I used narration, showing – and making the case that there had been – the development of an idea over a specific period, in a series of stages. I used compare and contrast in a paper on two different research traditions. I used process for a methods section. I learned that I would probably never write a causal analysis. Given the range of factors involved, the research techniques I use(d), and the underpinning assumptions about how knowledge is constructed, how could I provide evidence that something I did had an effect? For example, there are so many variables involved in writing development.

I learned from expert examples of these rhetorical modes: see Selzer (1981), for one of the best illustrations of literature review as classification, and I began to notice the modes in the books and articles I was reading for my PhD.

When I returned to the UK . . . there was nothing. No writing courses. No workshops. No writer's groups. No support for thesis writers. No discussion. Nothing. I developed a thesis writing course, since there seemed to be least resistance to the idea of 'teaching writing' at this point. Later, I developed courses for undergraduates – ranging from generic essay or report writing skills, to discipline-specific technical writing to dissertation writing. Then I started to work with academics on writing for publication. As research assessment began to bite, this topic was in demand, and it still is.

In some of these writing workshops and courses I introduce the rhetorical modes, briefly outlining each one and suggesting how we might use them in academic writing. I use examples, like Selzer (1981), and extracts from the journals participants are targeting to illustrate each mode. I wrote about the modes and used the Selzer (1981) example in my book *How to Write a Thesis* (Murray 2011b: Chapter 7). When I do rhetorical analysis in workshops, people – academics and researchers in various fields – say it opens their eyes to the 'secrets' of good writing.

The Rhetoric and Composition course was my introduction to the scholarship and research on writing. That is how I learned that writing was central to *my* learning – and my students' – that it could be learned and that it should be taught. I realised that while I had done very well in my undergraduate writing, in terms of passing exams, I had not learned how to use writing to construct my knowledge.

A module on academic writing

I drew on the literature covered in previous sections when I designed the module on Academic Writing for the postgraduate Certificate/Diploma course in Advanced Academic Studies at the University of Strathclyde (in Glasgow, UK).

The module ran in six three-hour seminars over three months. (See Appendix C for module aims, objectives, contents and assessment.) There were two routes for study in this module: (1) the role of writing in teaching and learning and (2) the role of writing in research. In course readings and at seminars we discussed both, but participants chose to focus on one for their studies and for their assignments.

I provided an overview of the wide range of literature on academic writing, and asked students to contextualise this literature in their disciplines throughout the module. The course readings went back as far as some of the early work in the Rhetoric and Composition tradition (Emig 1977). We covered some of the big names in the North American field (Elbow 1973, 1998; Boice 1987a, 1987b, 1990a) and a selection of UK studies by Hartley (1994, 2004), Lea and Street (1998) and Torrance *et al.* (1993). We read about the literacies approaches of Ivanic and Lea (2006) and Lillis (2001) and genre approaches, such as Swales (2004), and some of the early work in Australia, such as Lee and Boud (2003).

I also introduced a selection of literature on academic writing to show its range and have added to this selection for the purposes of this chapter, in order to bring it up to date (Black *et al.* 1998; Boice 1990a; Day 1996; Hartley 2008; Huff 1999; Moxley and Taylor 1997; Murray 2013b; Navarra 1998; Peat *et al.* 2002; Rodrigues 1997; Silvia 2007; Swales 2004; Sword 2012a, 2012b; Thomson and Kamler 2013; Thyer 1994; Wellington 2003; Williams and Coldron 1996; Zerubavel 1999).

Almost no one had come across any of this literature before. They could not be faulted for ignoring it, because they did not know it existed. In addition, some said they had not really given much thought to how writing is learned, which is not to say that they had neglected to think about it, but that they had never had an opportunity to discuss it before this module:

> The writing process was something I hadn't given much thought to before starting the course . . . One of the first topics explored was how is academic writing learned; the answer, certainly within the UK, seems to be by trial and error. On reflection I cannot recall being given formal instruction on the specifics of academic writing during my undergraduate career. This trial and error process was not just exclusively confined to academic writing, it extends to all forms of writing. For a skill that is so important, particularly in academic life, I am still surprised at how little time is given to formally developing writing techniques and the transference of those skills to students
>
> (Module participant quoted in Murray 2001: 35)

For some, these discussions revealed uncertainty about their own writing:

> I was very unsure of the writing process and was very nervous about committing to paper . . . I can remember the way in which my approach to writing changed as I read some of the theory on writing and adopted some of the ideas. I am now more confident of the structure and approach to writing an academic paper. However, I still have a long way to go.
>
> (Module participant quoted in Murray 2001: 35)

During the module we tried out a wide range of writing strategies, and we discussed how these might, or might not, be useful in our writing and/or for students' writing. We talked about how different strategies might work and whether they could overcome the challenges of writing.

This is where the resistance began. It was all well and good to present a range of literature, to browse a collection of textbooks and note that there was actually some empirical research, but trying out new writing strategies was different. Clearly, these discussions were interesting for exposing our assumptions and values, our writing knowledge and habits. Clearly, there was potential, theoretical benefit in having such discussions. Moreover, we agreed that it was important to experience new writing strategies first-hand, not just to read about them. We discussed whether or not these opportunities to write triggered shifts in perspective, from seeing writing as so bound up in the workings of the discipline that it could not and should not, for them, be separated out to seeing it as a 'skill' that needs developing.

We talked about whether we should see writing as a generic skill. We discussed the 'practical' approach – when I would attempt to reclaim the term 'practical' from the conceptual scrap heap where it is sometimes thrown. I wanted us to consider the specifics of writing practices. In this discussion we could compare our definitions of writing practices and descriptions of each other's actual writing practices. This discussion revealed the importance of gathering data on writing practices.

A theme in my contributions to these discussions was to flip the focus from our writing to our students' writing, or vice versa. For example, if we were talking about how useful it is to do some analysis of published journal articles, I would chip in that it might be equally useful for both undergraduate and postgraduates if we unpacked the structures of written arguments in our disciplines' journals, or if we defined what constitutes 'research' in some areas and if we explained what 'critique' meant by illustrating with examples. Almost any issue they raised, any writing strategies they found useful, prompted me to ask how it might apply for students. This meant that we were constantly making connections between the two strands of the module: our writing and our students' writing.

During the course I asked participants to do ten minutes of freewriting (Elbow 1973) twice a week and to email it to me. The purpose of this freewriting was to encourage them to try a strategy that has proved very useful to students but has been more challenging for lecturers. It also gave them a chance to reflect on what they were doing, and if they really hated freewriting – for whatever reason – they could write about that.

Interestingly, some did. There were a few who did not see the point of freewriting, did not see how it could be useful in academic writing, and, in fact, worried that it would make students' writing worse than it already was:

> I found, much to my surprise, that the freewriting excercises which were out of class (10 minutes twice a week) were much more difficult to complete. Indeed, I only managed to complete one of these exercises per week. . . . I suppose if nothing else the exercise of freewriting illustrated to me that this

method doesn't work for me, which in itself is useful to know. . . . There were various other aspects of the module that I found particularly useful in my writing. These include . . . goal setting and examining my writing habits. It has helped me gain . . . an insight into how I write and what methods of enhancing that process work and don't work for me.

This was in spite of the fact that we had read Elbow's rationale for and findings on the benefits of freewriting – that regular freewriting improves fluency – and students' accounts of how useful it is to be able to write at all, to write what they think and to overcome their fear of writing. In spite of this, some remained strongly, vociferously opposed to freewriting.

For the assessment, participants chose either to write about a teaching innovation involving students' writing or about a writing for publication project they were working on. They also wrote a thousand-word reflective piece on the writing process.

Their reflective writings focused on three themes: (1) writing development, or lack of it, (2) insights on the writing process and themselves as writers and (3) new uses of writing in teaching. For almost everyone, this was the first time they had written about their writing and about themselves as writers.

I collected and analysed their email communications over the course of a year, and analysed seminar discussions and written assignments (Murray 2002). This was a way of tracking responses to the course and to the writing strategies I had suggested. It also gave them a way of tracking their writing. What was clear from their emails and reflective writings was that learning about the scholarship and research on academic writing had been a revelation to them – literally.

Integrating research and teaching

Having said that these lecturers, and academics in general, were not knowledgeable about the literature on writing – and would have been quite comfortable owning up to that – it is my experience that they very quickly see the importance of paying more attention to the use of writing in their teaching once they had started to learn about it in the Academic Writing module described in the previous section (Murray 2001).

About halfway through the course I overheard participants talking about how they had tried out some of the new writing strategies in their teaching. In my experience, this was unusual: I thought it was unlikely that these participants would adopt new strategies so quickly, particularly when there had been such strong resistance to some of the strategies. They had chosen strategies that met students' needs. They made connections between current students' needs and their recent learning – with apologies if that sounds too obvious, but it doesn't always happen that way.

Participants told me about the techniques they were using to develop writing activities for their students. Surprisingly, given the scepticism about freewriting, that was one of the strategies they were using, although, interestingly, some said they did not use the term 'freewriting':

The . . . more surprising outcome is that I've found something I can do well, that works for me and that I can see taking forward, both as a tool for my personal writing, and as a method I will suggest to students to aid their writing. I have already suggested freewriting to a project student who was struggling with how to approach writing his report. I did not give it a name, but merely suggested that he should write down the topics he wanted to cover in each section, and then write down everything he wanted to cover in each section, and then write down everything he knew about that topic for five minutes, without considering structure or punctuation. Then to go through with his highlighter pen and pick out the useful bits and use them as bullet points for his final write up. His feedback has been very positive, so I think that one will be used again.

(Murray 2001: 36)

In my analysis of all their reflective writings seven strategies introduced in the module seemed to have most impact on their writing and/or teaching:

1   discussing writing with others;
2   getting feedback on writing from others;
3   freewriting (Elbow 1973);
4   generative writing (Boice 1990a);
5   goal setting for writing;
6   using a framework for writing abstracts (Brown 1994/95);
7   discussing writing with the course tutor (Murray 2001: 37).

Five months after they had completed the module I interviewed them to find out if they were still using these strategies, and they said they were. They explained how they had adopted writing activities for teaching purposes:

- helping students to think about writing processes;
- enabling students to assess their learning;
- promoting active learning;
- as a mechanism for students to integrate classes (Murray 2001: 39).

Participants saw relationships between writing and teaching:

My writing has changed. I'm writing more and I'm writing better. I've gone from writing nothing to writing something. I review my writing more. I get students to think about their writing more.

I use writing in class as a dynamic: writing in different forms, with different purposes, linking back to the assignment, summing up, making links. Also with dissertation students: we discuss and I prompt them to write there and then. Therefore I'm much more assertive in saying, 'Shouldn't you be writing that down?'

(Murray 2001: 39)

That last comment could be misinterpreted as encouraging verbatim note-taking, but, of course, it means something completely different here.

Would this have happened if they had not attended this module for some formal 'tuition' in writing? Would they have seen these relationships between their writing and their students'? Would they have gone on to use new approaches to writing if they had just read about them? It is likely that the seminar discussions, cutting across disciplinary boundaries, provided opportunities for participants to contextualise writing strategies in their disciplines and in their writing. In this sense, and to this extent, they had opportunities to form new relationships between their writing and their knowledge, and to think about how their students might do so too.

Conclusion

My approaches to academic writing draw on different traditions, traditions developed in different higher education cultures: Rhetoric and Composition, academic writing development and the growing literature on writing groups and retreats for academics and professionals (Aitchison and Guerin 2014; Grant and Knowles 2000; Jackson 2009).

The Academic Writing module introduced participants to a range of approaches to the theory and practice of academic writing, while always using social writing activities. By their own admission it opened their eyes to the world of writing research and challenged some of their assumptions about writing. It provided answers to questions about writing skills and strategies and, to some extent, gave them time and space to begin to put new strategies into practice.

The components of social writing involved in becoming rhetorical are:

- learning from others, as we discuss writing knowledge and practice;
- talking about writing with those at earlier stages in writing (students and emerging researchers) to develop understanding – theirs and ours; and
- developing relationships between knowledge, knowledge production, writing practices and teaching and learning.

In my view, the Academic Writing module was a necessary, but perhaps not sufficient step in the development of social writing for course members. It provided the knowledge base and theoretical backdrop, and kept an explicit link to participants' writing and teaching practices, but it did not guarantee the writing development of everyone. Writing is not merely a series of lessons; it is made up of negotiations and interactions, and the capacity to engage in these negotiations varies from time to time and from person to person.

The next chapter takes up this point. It explores modes of writing development that draw on this literature and that help those who participate in such courses put it into practice. The focus is therefore on developing individual writing skills in workshops run on social writing lines.

Chapter 4

Skill

In this chapter I describe workshops and courses for developing writing skills. I do not spend a lot of time describing the writing activities, since I have covered those in detail elsewhere (Murray 2013b). Instead, in this chapter I will argue that discussion with others who write can play a role in developing writing skills. Yes, it is about developing writing skills – and that may be an essential step in the early stages of becoming a writer – but it is not just about individual skill. The individual writer can use social processes to develop writing skills. In case this seems too obvious, I should say that developing writing skills in these ways is not the norm in workplaces and researcher or professional development programmes. This means that any obvious benefits will not be available to everyone, which is why, I think, the argument is still worth making.

Key messages

- There is a case for formal and informal (continuous) learning through writing workshops and courses.
- This means developing the skill of writing in different ways, in different spaces and at different times and trying out different strategies at different stages in our writing process.
- Discussing writing at each stage is one way to develop skill in writing.

Am I saying that any writing is good writing? Am I ignoring the question of 'quality' in writing? It may seem so, but that is not my point. My proposition is that the process of writing can be broken down into numerous stages, and that doing so is helpful. Moreover, the activities described in this chapter will – taken together – develop a decent draft:

1   writing a sentence defining the main purpose of the article;
2   doing some freewriting and generative writing on that to develop and focus the idea;

3   checking with the editor that the subject and purpose of the article are relevant for a specific journal;
4   analysing articles published recently in that journal and working out how to relate the article to at least one published there recently;
5   drafting the abstract;
6   sketching a detailed outline.
7   addressing anticipated critiques in the article.

In any case, for those who do these seven writing tasks and are also using strategies and conversations proposed in this chapter to write regularly, there is likely to be some 'quality' in their first draft. Clearly, that draft will need to be revised, probably many times. Clearly, they will get feedback, perhaps from many different readers. Clearly, they can then incrementalise the revisions, just as they incrementalised the writing. However, this chapter does not reduce writing to a linear series of simple, discrete steps; instead, it shows that an essential component of writing is interacting with other writers, making the case that this is a key writing 'skill'.

This chapter argues that writing skill can develop through social writing. It describes how different strategies can be combined to create productive writing processes. It draws on participants' reactions to the introduction of these strategies and their reports on using them over the longer term. As with all the chapters in this book, the emphasis is not on the individual writer – though many individual voices are included here – but on the development of individuals' skills through interactions with others who write.

This social approach may be particularly useful in the current context of competitive writing (or it may seem to run against the grain of current writing cultures). One of the side effects of research assessment has arguably been the erosion of cooperative, collaborative writing. Yes, major grants are still collaborative in nature. Yes, many written outputs from such grants are multi-authored and, perhaps, collaboratively written. But most academics and researchers will not have such big grants, and even those who do may not know how to use social processes to increase productivity and reduce the pressure of writing.

'It's okay to say, I don't know how to do this'

Many will disagree with this statement – a quotation from an interview conducted with a participant in one of my first writing groups. Some will wonder, what is someone who doesn't know how to write doing in an academic or professional job? How can they do their job if they don't know how to write well? Some will argue that once you have the skill, you have all you need, but my argument is that skill alone will not necessarily lead to writing. Writing skill is a – perhaps *the* – necessary but not sufficient prerequisite for writing well and often.

The person who said, 'It's okay to say I don't know how to do this' was very clear that writing for publication meant writing in a new genre, and that this implied that there was learning to be done. The interview was actually focused on finding out about experiences of a writer's group, and her responses outlined the kinds of learning she felt she had to do, even though English was her discipline:

So the writer's group definitely enabled you to have strategies that you could use.

Absolutely and I would say that even despite the fact that I'm an English teacher, so I taught children writing. Writing was one of the things I was very interested in, and it was the topic of my PhD, so I did know a lot about writing. So I was probably an extreme case. I wasn't a typical case who was coming to a writer's group not knowing about writing. I knew a great deal about writing, but I still found I was actually having to learn a new genre of writing that no one had ever taught me.

That is interesting, and that genre was academic writing?

Yes, and it is a genre. It has its conventions and strategies and genre markers, which make it unlike any other kind of writing. So the writer's group helped me with that.

Can you give me an example?

One of the things I thought was, okay, I don't know how academic writing works, so I would go to articles, and I would read them to see how they worked, e.g. how does an abstract work, what are the language features of an abstract? When you're structuring the writing, if you look at the big picture, if you look at the overall structure, then it is like telling a story. It has got a beginning, a middle and an end. But then I learned that even within the genre of academic writing there are different genres . . . So I was trying to look at the language features of how it worked, to help me copy that style and develop my own academic style.

That is really interesting, and maybe that's why a lot of people think academics should know how to write for journals and academia.

Absolutely!

But you're saying it is actually a different genre?

So I had to learn something that was totally new to me, and it is something that I've actually offered in [my institution] to other departments who complain about students' essays: 'So have you taught them how to write that kind of essay?' And the assumption is that they would have learned that in school, and they haven't. If you want them to write an academic essay you have to teach them, not just the content of that essay, but you have to teach them how to present an argument, because often in school they would have been told to do a discussion where they've been given pros and cons, but not an argument, and I think that goes for all the way through to students and academics themselves. They don't know how that kind of writing works, and they have a great lack of confidence because they feel it is their fault. They should know, and I don't think they should, and that is why I think the writer's group helped me so much because it was an acknowledgment that you are an academic, you are a bright person, you're good at your job, you know a lot about the subject, but you don't actually know how to communicate it to people in the generic form that is acceptable for journals, so you have to learn that, and that is okay. It is okay to say I don't know how to do this.

She proposes links to school education – not finding fault, but pointing to the gap between school writing and professional or academic writing. She defines the crisis of confidence that many smart, competent people have when it comes to academic writing. She points to assumptions we make about how writing skills develop – assumptions that are not routinely interrogated or refreshed. She argued that the need for writing skills was not only her individual development need but a more general need, and that it would be useful if people could own up to their need for skills development.

Learning writing skills can be seen as learning how to involve others in our writing, understanding the role that others can play both in our skills development and in our writing, and involving others in the development of our research and our arguments. Writing can involve a shift in identity – from practitioner to researcher, for example, or from doctoral student to published researcher – and working with others can facilitate this shift.

Learning writing skills at a workshop

This section outlines a workshop for developing writing skills (see Appendix D for programme) and explains how skills development and social writing are interrelated.

This workshop is designed for those who are starting to write for publication, and it has also been used by those who were already publishing and wanted to boost their writing and productivity. The aim is to introduce a range of writing strategies and help participants see how they can combine them in a coherent, managed process – that is, a process 'managed' by themselves.

The activities in this workshop are based on established theory and research, which can be summarised as two sets of very different approaches: 'structured' and 'freewheeling'. The structured approach involves targeting an audience, analysing the content of articles in order to define its requirements, for example, in order to construct the kinds of structure and style that are required. The freewheeling approach involves developing ideas *through* writing and attending to structure at a later stage.

Each of us is likely to have a preference for or tendency towards one or the other – structurers will not start writing without an outline; freewheelers will absolutely start writing without an outline – but it may be useful to use both strategies. I see developing writing 'skill', therefore, not just as learning technical skills – paragraphing, sentencing and grammar – but as, in part, a process of adopting new strategies and integrating them with existing ones. A key proposition for participants to think about and try out during this workshop is, therefore, how to change how they write: instead of using either structured or freewheeling approaches, to use both.

Engaging with this concept – which will be new to most, in the sense that they may never have thought about their writing in this way – involves talking about the writing activities they try in this workshop: for each writing activity, they talk about how the activity produced text for their writing projects, what they think about that way of producing text and what they think about that text.

In this workshop each approach to writing – each component of the skill of writing – involves a writing activity. After each activity there is a discussion. The activities are outlined in detail elsewhere (Murray 2013b): for example, the five-minute 'warm up' for writing is designed to get participants to focus on what they *want* to write about, to write about that and to discuss their intentions and/or aspirations with another writer in the workshop. For all of them, writing about their writing in this way is likely to be novel. Talking about their writing at such an early stage is not routine either. For anyone in the workshop who has not yet written for publication, there is often relief that they managed to write anything at all in five minutes. The 'skill' of writing, in this context, is therefore about identifying personal motivations and articulating and consolidating them in these conversations, while starting to generate text.

In the next phase of the workshops we analyse examples of published writing, ideally from journals that they plan to target. This involves, for example, analysing the first sentences of abstracts, to identify how the problematic is established, and the last sentence, to identify how the contribution is defined, and looking at how the two are interrelated in many different ways in many different published articles. We look at the use of verb forms to define the purposes of articles: 'This article reviews . . . analyses . . . explores . . . offers'. This kind of analysis develops participants' skills in analysing writing, and this, in turn, works as a prompt for their writing. For example, writing sentences that identify the main purpose of their articles is another five-minute writing activity, followed by discussion. In this way, writing skills are developed, and discussion is a chance to process the approach and think about the text they produced and how they are going to develop the idea and the text.

We also discuss the idea of emailing editors with a pre-submission inquiry. Not everyone agrees with this – surely this is an imposition? Who are we to contact editors, especially when we haven't even written the article yet? We discuss the pros and cons, including the cost of finding out that it is not relevant after having shaped the article for a specific journal – and the reticence that some feel about sending the email, even once they have written it in the workshop. Is this about lack of confidence? Is it lack of confidence in their ability to write the article, or is it lack of confidence in the quality of their writing? Or is it about not quite seeing themselves as writers yet? This is an important discussion, in developing motivation, and writing the email is useful in focusing and deciding what the main point of the paper will be.

The next step is to try freewriting (Elbow 1973) and generative writing (Boice 1990a) – for many, these are new activities, and for structurers they can seem to lack purpose because they prefer to have a structure before they start writing. Many, however, say that they develop their ideas more freely using these strategies. In pairs, they discuss what they think and feel about the process of writing this way and the text they produced. Group discussion reveals different uses of freewriting and generative writing – different purposes and products – and specific ways in which they can be used to develop ideas, focus thinking and produce text.

Then we use a series of prompts to draft abstracts. Discussion and feedback focus on this as a strategy for drafting and on the text produced. This twenty- or thirty-minute writing task – plus twenty minutes' discussion – is used to clarify the main line of the argument and to revise.

In these activities, therefore, participants not only generate text, but also give and receive feedback on the process and product. In these discussions participants learn about each other's research, hear generally positive responses to their research and writing and initiate discussions of their research and writing, discussions that often continue after the workshop.

The next activity shifts from generating text to creating structure: developing a detailed outline for the whole article. This involves three levels of outlining: defining writing goals, sub-goals and sub-sub-goals in terms of sections and sub-sections of the article, and setting word limits for each. This integrates with the draft abstract, as sentences from the abstract can be linked to – or repeated, with elaboration – in the main body of the article. Sketching and discussing outlines is a way of rehearsing the structure of the whole argument.

We then look at examples of reviewers' feedback: common reasons why papers are rejected, examples of reviews and a process for dealing with and responding to peer review. Discussion focuses on negative reviews, reviewers' focus on methodology, in particular, and on the apparent trend towards contradictory reviews. We discuss why reviews are contradictory, why some reviewers are vindictive and how it feels to receive negative reviews and rejections.

If this is beginning to seem like group therapy, there may be no harm in that, if it helps participants work through the negative associations of this step in the writing process. Perhaps more importantly, it can help them to anticipate critiques and strengthen their articles accordingly. That this happens in a non-review discussion is important – yes, their work will be subject to peer review, but no, that need not be a destructive process. Of course, reviews focus on individual, often single-authored papers, but that does not mean processing reviews has to be a solitary process.

At this stage in this workshop, participants are likely to be thinking about the process of talking about writing explicitly, if they haven't already. Many describe the benefits of talking about writing: clarifying, focusing, building confidence – we are all in the same boat. This opens up a range of ways to use discussion to progress writing.

This is the final topic in the workshop. We talk about strategies to sustain writing over the long term: writing retreats, writer's groups, writing meetings and micro-groups (all covered in other chapters of this book).

The final task is setting goals and sub-goals, including thinking about how to continue to use strategies learned in this workshop.

This workshop therefore develops a range of skills, showing how to use writing activities and conversations, not just to review learning, but also to progress writing and thinking. While the focus of the workshop is on skills development, social processes are used throughout. Developing skill in writing in this way involves developing social skills for writing. Clearly, not everyone will talk about every stage of their writing in this way for every project, but these participants will be able to do so, whenever they think it will be useful and feasible.

However, will this only be possible among those who developed these social writing skills? Will others know what freewriting or writing to prompts means? Will they see the value of talking about writing-in-progress in these ways? Perhaps. Perhaps not. Perhaps extending the skills development process of this workshop to a longer period would increase integration of these new strategies in a range of settings and with a range of other people?

Learning writing skills at a course

This section describes a six-month Writing for Publication course, which ran the skills development activities of the workshop described in the previous section over a longer period.

This course involved a three-hour meeting every month (see Appendix E for programme). This gave participants much more time to develop their ideas, do some reading and, theoretically, more writing. In practice, it was not as simple as that: the difficulty of finding writing time and space to write between the course meetings persisted. This was why I started to put such an emphasis on goal setting and monitoring – key skills often used for other activities, but also applicable to, though less familiar in, the writing process. Feedback and evaluation showed that this course had many benefits for participants, including getting published (Hislop *et al.* 2008, Morss and Murray 2001). However, the problem of lack of time for writing remained.

During the six-month course I tried to help participants to sustain social interactions with other writers by setting up a 'buddy' system, where they met regularly with one or more other course participants, and this seemed to work:

> It gives you support and encouragement in order to keep going, and if you have a buddy that you either met up with or you communicated with, just to kind of keep the ball rolling, stimulate you to keep up.

However, the social interactions that were introduced in the course were difficult and often impossible to sustain in a range of workplaces. We set up a mentoring scheme to try to increase peer discussion of writing-in-progress, but this became a burden on the mentors, who themselves were struggling to make progress with their writing:

It was a bit of a constraint for me, I think, because it deflected from my own writing, and I wasn't coming to the mentorship group to do my own writing. I felt I was responsible for holding the group together.

They all found it difficult to find a time to meet to write:

Trying to get six professionals who all work in completely different fields together at lunch time – it just didn't happen.

Consequently, after completing the course none of the participants used the mentoring system. We encouraged participants to talk about their writing with colleagues and to meet to write, in the way that they had during this course, but there was a language barrier between those who had been at the course and those who had not. They had different concepts and behaviours. They defined writing in different ways.

As one participant put it, the Writing for Publication course had been an idealised environment. It protected writing and writers. It provided dedicated writing time – one hour of writing at each three-hour meeting – which was not possible in other environments, even when management gave 'permission' for writing and where writing was part of the main business of the institution, such as in universities and some clinical workplaces. Some spoke of feeling that they had to 'sneak writing in' to their workplaces. Others were worried that they would be seen as 'skiving' if they were writing at work. The problem, for some, was that writing for publication was seen as benefiting the writer, rather than improving patient care, the student experience or professional practice, or creating new knowledge.

Two years after the completion of one of these courses, I went back to participants to ask them about their writing practices. One of the themes that came up in interviews was the need to change writing behaviours, and the specific change that they all talked about more than anything else was writing in shorter increments of time – 'snack writing', they called it.

'Snack writing'

The idea of breaking writing down into sub-tasks – or 'snacks' – seemed to have been extremely helpful. They all remembered this, and they all said that 'snack writing' helped them most – and not just for writing, but also for other tasks too, for both research and professional tasks.

Defining writing in terms of small increments meant that it could be 'snacked', and that when they did not define their writing task in terms of small increments, it would require a 'binge'. For example, most workshop participants wrote between 100 and 200 words in the five-minute activities, and if their article were outlined in terms of 200-word blocks, they could see how to create time slots to do that writing. If they did not, there was a chance that they would not write at all, because the writing tasks would be too large, and the blocks of time required for such large tasks were simply not available.

Having said all that, there is often uncertainty about whether or not snack writing will produce 'good writing', and the discussions in writing workshops and courses play an important role in airing these uncertainties, while acknowledging that questions about the quality of the writing they do in this way can be reconfigured as just another component of writing. Like any other component of writing, it can be managed through social processes.

Nor should we forget about those who say they cannot snack write because they need much longer periods of time to really think and concentrate. Some said they tried snack writing, but it did not work for them. Others say they thought they would never do it, but found it more useful than they expected. As with every strategy, it is, of course, important to think of snack writing not as the only way, but as one of many ways to write, and it can be used in different ways and for different purposes, as the following quotations show.

Participants said that snack writing helped them to stop and start writing quickly and make better use of the time they had for writing, rather than looking for more time to write. Furthermore, in these quotations their use of specific timeframes suggests a shift in conceptualisations of writing time:

> I had a date for publication of my article, so the snacking did really help, and it was surprising how quickly you could get into it and pick it up again, and that's maybe what scared me. I always though, no, I will have to sit for at least three-quarters of an hour before I get my brain around and into it, but the fact is you could come in and out quickly.

> The thing that sticks in my mind is this idea of snacking. You don't have to sit for forty-eight hours writing something up. Do it in half-an-hour and plan the time. Commit yourself to a timetable . . . that very simple technique of breaking it right down was useful.

It helped them to write more regularly and more freely:

> I think now what I would do is, I would put aside time every week, and then I would try and use the structure to work on bits of it, so that you are working your way through it, snacking on it. . . . Just write freely and then review it after.

It meant they could adapt time slots that were not designated for writing and be opportunistic in their writing:

> sometimes [people] don't turn up, or they finish early. It would be good to have an extra ten minutes where I can sit and get my work out, and that was something I used throughout the course.

The thing that really sticks with me and that I do use is 'snacking'. So, you know, that having some time and thinking, 'Right, I've got this piece of work to do, I've got space, I'll start', and then leave it and come back to it, and it is amazing how it starts to fill up.

It provided a way of fitting writing in with other activities:

Writing had to be fitted in between everything else – kids, family, whatever, and you are just not in the mood to write. So then you just think, I will put this off till later. But knowing that you are able just to write what is on your mind at the time, and then you can go and do something else, was a technique I had never used before . . . It was either I can do this in the next three hours, or I cannot do any of it because it's really hard to get into it.

This developed their self-efficacy and confidence – possible prerequisites for writing but certainly required for behaviour change:

It took away the fear, but it also made me have a bit of belief in myself. Before [the Writing for Publication] course I hadn't written anything apart from my undergraduate essays . . . I had never felt I was any good at it, and maybe I'm still not [laughs]. At least I now realise I can do it, and I definitely think the course was responsible for that.

They also used snacking for other tasks, not just for writing:

I took it on board to be personally . . . to be a very broad thing, so that it was about losing the fear of writing, actually being able to contribute to news weekly or the team briefing or even writing patient reports or something like that. You know, suddenly it wasn't just a huge task anymore.

However, while snack writing could work in these ways, and while it did help them progress their writing projects and other tasks, their writing programme often broke down on return to the workplace:

The only time I've ever got any meaningful writing done, was having allocated time out, sort of the permission thing.

I agree with everything you say about motivating [to participant 1], prioritising, but it also about the [institution] saying . . . well there should be some actual time that is allocated.

it goes back to what you were saying [to another participant] about completely having ring-fenced time, whatever you want to call it, where you have got clear things that you are going to produce and deliver within that time, but to negotiate it with your line manager.

This suggests that there is a need for perceived and actual support to privilege writing in workplaces. Or it might tell us something about how they were using snack writing. Snack writing is less likely to work if writers have not defined 'writing' in terms of increments that can be written in short periods of time. If the writing sub-tasks are all still long – e.g. 1500 words – and if that task is not defined in terms of sub-sub-tasks, then it will be difficult and probably impossible to snack write it, even if the writer has practised snack writing before.

This is where social writing can play a role: when writers remind each other of these principles. This is especially valuable when writers are feeling overwhelmed by a writing task, which may be less about the demands of the writing task itself than about the writer's sense of the difficulty of finding time to do it. The difficulty may lie in the process of making time to write, more than in the task itself, although in reality it is often difficult to tease out this distinction. This is a problem that can be addressed in social writing. At the very least, writers can remind each other of these principles and restore a sense of agency in managing the writing process and its challenges:

> Writing is a process that can be actively manipulated and controlled. It seems pretty silly now, given the many ways in which successful writing is important to a research scientist, that I wasn't previously more active in working out how to do it within the constraints of the job.

This point reminds us that suggesting that writers manage their time better or build up their sense of individual agency in relation to writing will seem like over-simplifications. Writing is not a series of fixed events; there is a set of dynamic processes that generate writing. These can involve interactions and relationships with others. That academic writing is a different genre, that writing is a process and that the process can be structured and managed – all of this can be learned in workshops and courses, but it can be sustained through interactions with others who write.

Actively managing the writing process

The workshop and course described in this chapter suggest two ways to develop writing skills. While the theoretical underpinning of these interventions and the evidence of their impact is provided elsewhere, the process of actively managing the writing process is a skill in itself, a skill that may have to be learned or adapted from other activities.

We do use strategies like 'snacking' with other tasks. With research, for example, most people will have a schedule of work, defined sub-goals and deadlines, will have reviewed these with whoever they report to or are accountable to – such as funders – but not so much with writing. There will, of course, be an imperative to write up and publish findings, perhaps in a range of forms, but the sub-goals for doing that, and the interim deadlines for each task, are less likely to be defined in the same way or to the same extent. Why is that?

Is writing so different from other activities that is must be planned and managed in a different way? Is it so 'creative' that it must not be tied down to the same linear processes as other tasks? Is the process so complex that it simply cannot be defined? Why is it that we use goal setting and monitoring for other tasks in our professional and personal lives, but not with writing? This is, of course, a sweeping generalisation: perhaps it is only people who come to my workshops and groups who experience writing as a challenge, but there are enough of them to suggest this subject must be addressed.

Perhaps everyone else *is* actively managing their writing? I do not think so. There is no data to persuade me that writing is easily and routinely actively managed. Instead, it seems to me that it is more likely to be experienced as disjointed, disarticulated from other academic and professional tasks and even, for some, as chaotic. In some settings, where the act of writing is not discussed at all, this may even be the default position. How common this is, I cannot be sure. What I do know is that moving from that disarticulated experience to actively managing writing need not take long and need not be laborious. In fact, I have heard many academics and professionals wondering aloud why they did not take control of their writing earlier. Now *that* is an interesting question, and it leads to very interesting conversations.

Perhaps the problem has been that strategies for actively managing writing are not solely solitary, although they have often been presented as individualist or individualised. As long as there are no interactions or relationships around writing some may find that actively managing their writing is impossible. Actively managing writing means integrating it in our lives. This happens *through* interactions and relationships.

'It's not earth-shattering, is it?'

This was a comment from someone who had just participated in one of my Writing for Publication workshops. Yes, he said, my workshop had been very useful, very practical, but there was nothing 'earth-shattering' about it. His view was that all the points I made in the workshop and in this chapter were obvious, and that academic writing was, indeed, as straightforward a process as I had depicted it to be.

Obviously, writing will happen and our writing will develop if we write regularly and in different ways. Obviously, it is useful to talk to others about our writing, as we write. Obviously, we can change our writing behaviours so as to be more productive. Of course we can combine different strategies to create our own personal writing process: combining both structuring and freewheeling. What is not so obvious is how we might do all that.

Bright, hardworking people still struggle to write what they want or as often as they want. The experiences of participants in Writing for Publication workshops and courses suggest that it is useful to develop writing skills: learning about strategies for generating text and understanding how academic writing works.

Some of this understanding develops in discussions with others. Some of the skill development occurs through such discussions.

> The components of social writing involved in writing workshops are:
>
> - defining academic writing skills in discussions with others who write;
> - discussing writing plans, aspirations and motivations – not fixating on barriers; and
> - reflecting on, critiquing and integrating new knowledge – about research and writing – through conversations with others who write.

In practice, of course, sometimes we write with others and sometimes we write in solitude. But could social writing learning also have an impact on our solitary writing?

The Writing for Publication workshops and courses described in this chapter developed social writing skills. What they did not do – because we were not aware of the need for it at the time – was develop social writing skills in a way that participants could manage for themselves after the workshop or course. They had not learned the skill of constructing social relations around writing at work. There was something missing, therefore, from their writing skill. One solution was to provide longer periods of dedicated writing time, with longer periods of contact between writers, to see if this would help. An obvious solution was writing retreats, the subject of the next chapter.

Chapter 5

Structure

My earlier studies, discussed in previous chapters, showed the value of social processes in writing, coupled with formal learning about academic writing, but in each study there was evidence of limitations to the benefits of these approaches. For example, while it helped to have peer support, and while it was useful to understand the construction of written arguments, there was no guarantee that these – together or separately – would lead to regular writing. In fact, there was evidence of problems with making time and space to write, to the extent that writing was not routinely possible in a range of workplaces.

In the context of current workplace cultures, therefore, the place of writing is problematic. In order to address this problem, I developed a way to privilege writing – a writing-only environment – so that people could put their knowledge about writing into practice. At writing retreats there is almost nothing but time and space for writing. This may sound like a rejection of workplace settings, but it is a way to provide concrete support for writing.

The main argument of this chapter is that a structured writing retreat is a way of working. It is not only a way of developing as a writer. It is not only a way of developing good writing habits and – to quote many participants – 'discipline' in writing, but a way of writing throughout a career and continuing to develop through writing. This approach is powerful *because* it builds research- and writing-oriented conversations and relationships.

Key messages

- Structured writing retreats create time and space for writing.
- Conversations about writing become conversations about research.
- Structured writing retreats and micro-groups are ways to do research.

This chapter explains how a structured writing retreat develops the habits of social writing, increasing written outputs and the time available for writing. Participants' views are included to show not only how they benefit from the model, but also how they adapt it to writing in their disciplinary cultures, work environments and other venues, such as cafés and home. Initially, research suggested that skills and strategies developed at retreats could not be transferred to other settings (Murray and Newton 2008), but now it seems that they can (Murray 2014).

Writing retreat models

I just wish I had done it earlier. I had it in my mind that retreat was a last resort – I thought, surely I can just get on with it. But I see now that it's much more productive

A writing retreat is an obvious way to make time and space for writing. It provides dedicated writing time. People who attend retreats regularly over a period of a year or so say that this changes their writing habits and makes them write and publish more. A retreat is not so much a 'last resort' as a way of becoming a more productive writer.

There are three types of retreat: the so-called 'solitary confinement' model, where people write all day in solitude in separate rooms, the 'typing pool' model, where they all write in the same room and the 'hybrid', which is a bit of both. All three have been shown to benefit writers and researchers in a range of institutions and disciplines (Grant and Knowles 2000; Grant 2006; Moore 2003; Moore et al. 2010; Murray and Newton 2009).

Any retreat has its own format, often according to participants' needs, but they probably share some or all of the following purposes:

- privileging writing over everything else;
- legitimising the act of writing in academic and professional work;
- developing the discipline of writing;
- inducing the level of concentration needed for academic writing;
- stimulating discussion of research and writing;
- enhancing writing behaviours, concepts and relationships;
- linking discipline, behaviours and concentration;
- increasing/improving outputs for research assessment/promotion.

The question of why writing might need to be 'legitimised' was addressed in earlier chapters: while everyone may agree that writing is – or should be – a legitimate academic or professional activity, it is not always experienced that way. There are numerous accounts in my studies and elsewhere of how other tasks routinely challenge the legitimacy of academic writing.

The core principles of a writing retreat are that there is dedicated writing time, without interruptions and without the threat of interruptions, which, for some, is not available either at home or at work. This is also non-surveillance, in the sense that participants' outputs are not measured. There is ample measuring of outputs in other settings.

However, some see retreats as a remedial intervention for those who do not or cannot write, and assume that once you have been to one retreat you will not 'need' to attend any more. This view is illustrated by comments I have heard – and heard about – at various universities:

> Retreats are for people at an early stage in their research careers, who need that boost to their confidence.

This view sees writing retreats as instrumental, and it is true that they generate outputs for research assessments. However, to see them as only having that function, or only providing retreats when research assessment is looming, is to miss out on potential benefits of regular retreats over a longer period. Nor do structured writing retreats only benefit early career researchers. Of course, there are benefits in attending retreats at that stage, but there are ongoing benefits from attending throughout a career. For example, a well-published academic recently said to me that he was, 'relieved to see that [he] could still write'. This suggests that retreats have benefit for experienced writers, particularly those with management responsibilities. (For more on balancing competing priorities see Chapter 8.)

Unlike other types of group writing that include giving and receiving feedback on writing (Caffarella and Barnett 2000), the exclusive focus on writing at structured retreats means that participants do not have to think about feedback, but can focus on generating text. This is not to say that feedback on writing is not important, but that there are benefits in focusing on writing without feedback. In practice, many participants give and receive feedback to and from me and to and from each other. Retreat participants do not, therefore, avoid feedback, but the focus is on writing.

The 'typing pool'

I developed the typing pool model for a retreat I was running at a university in Australia. Because the Australian government was introducing research assessment in Australia at that time, we had senior officers dropping in throughout the writing day to explain the assessment process, describe the institutional strategy, answer questions and so on. At the same time, we were at a writing retreat, and everyone wanted to get on with their writing.

If we had all been writing in separate rooms, we would have had to round everybody up and move them into one room for each briefing and then back to their writing rooms after the briefing, but if we all wrote in the same room, this would be less time-consuming and disruptive. Because we all stayed in the same room, we were able to pause in our writing, listen to the briefing, have the discussion and then get right back to writing.

From this, I went on to create the format that is now called a structured writing retreat. At the time, and in feedback collected afterwards, I realised that it worked quite well (Murray and Cunningham 2011), and now it is clear from participants' more recent accounts that writing collectively in this way works very well. The fixed structure of the retreat day is key. (See Appendix F for a structured writing retreat programme.)

Social writing at these retreats involves the development of tacit relationships with others who are writing:

> peer group pressure in the nicest sense that can kick us into action . . . There's nothing quite like seeing somebody in the room across from you working away to push you into keeping up.

> looking up and seeing other people writing was like doing some team-work, although everyone was working on their own project . . . I felt 'pulled in'.

If this seems like an obvious way to privilege writing, it should be noted that it is not the norm in most workplaces to write in this way. If it seems obvious that using this schedule will produce lots of writing, it should be noted that most participants are astonished at how much they can achieve in eleven hours over two days. They are relieved to see that they can write all day, be highly productive and have the evening off.

The next three sections highlight recurring themes in people's accounts of this form of social writing, showing how participants felt that they had made personal changes in this social writing setting.

Changing practices

Anyone who goes to a structured writing retreat is likely to have already committed to writing. They may not have decided to change their writing practices, but they have decided to try what is, for most, a new way of writing.

In discussions, it then becomes clear that people are thinking about why this structure works for them. There are usually plenty of reflections on their usual writing habits – those that work and those that do not. Perhaps, therefore, those who choose to go to these retreats are predisposed to changing their writing practices?

In any case, it is clear that people do change their concepts, practices and behaviours at structured writing retreats. They do articulate what these changes are, and they do voice aspirations to maintain them after retreat. Specifically, many plan to write in shorter increments of time, to write more often and to write with others. Structured writing retreats are therefore a way to do the kinds of snack writing (discussed in the previous chapter) that can be instrumental in getting started in writing and writing regularly. Using snack writing over two days at a structured writing retreat is an opportunity to embed the strategy in practice, and the discussions provide opportunities to consider how to do this after a retreat.

Spacing and pacing

Everyone is looking for space and time to write. With very few exceptions everyone would be happy with more writing time. The structure of a writing retreat delineates specific periods of time for writing and discussing writing, and it also creates a space for thinking about writing. This structure holds the boundaries and helps to develop pacing, in the sense of defining increments of writing. Again, the group effect makes this easier to achieve.

Spacing and pacing – as opposed to the headlong rush to write and the fear of stopping (in case you cannot start writing again) – are imposed by the fixed programme. At retreats, and even more so over multiple retreats, people learn what writing they can do in specific timeslots. They learn how to pace themselves, and this includes taking time to review progress and set new goals. It also includes making time to talk about writing-in-progress – as part of the writing process. Therefore, while they are writing all day, they do so in a paced manner, with regular breaks.

For many, this is a revelation. They compare it to the urgency and stress of un-paced writing. They compare the focused retreat space with the overwhelming busy-ness of workplaces. They compare cooperative conversations at retreats with hostilities and degradations – not an exaggeration – in workplaces. They see that previous failures to write relate to workplace cultures and the invisibility of writing in those cultures. Sharing experiences and seeing commonalities between them is a key component of this change in perspective.

Routine and discipline

It comes as no surprise that this structure, with its fixed programme, is found to instil discipline. This comes up all the time. Everyone recognises the need for discipline in writing, but most have previously had no way to develop it.

However, a very small minority see this approach as mechanistic. How can you decide, in advance, what you want to write? Surely we use writing to work out what we think and what we want to say? Why should you stop writing once you've started, just because the programme or facilitator says you should? Why not just keep going for as long as you can or until you've finished something? Why not be flexible and go with the flow of writing?

Routine and discipline, so often defined in terms of personal qualities or deficiencies, are clearly developed in social writing. The fixed time slots and the group's commitment to the programme help to develop persistence. This is not just about accommodating the needs of a group – though that is part of it – but about finding out something new about our writing processes through social writing: that we can create routine and discipline in our writing.

Routine and discipline are not, therefore, stifling creativity and flow; there are so many epiphanies and breakthroughs in writing at these retreats, and flow and creativity are not possible if we do not write. In fact, perhaps we should no longer think of creativity and discipline as contraries.

Outputs

Almost all the time in a structured writing programme is spent writing. This usually produces significant outputs, in terms of journal articles drafted or revised for
resubmission, PhD chapters drafted or revised or research proposals drafted or
submitted. Here is an example of a set of typical outputs produced at one retreat
in eleven hours over two days by one group of nine people:

- Outlined research proposal (300 words), PhD studentship application
  (300 words), drafted and revised conference abstract (150 words) and
  short paper (1000 words), drafted proposal for a small grant (1000 words).
- Wrote introduction of PhD thesis (6000 words) plus generated lots of
  ideas for the chapter and other chapters.
- Achieved short-term goal of getting started writing for PhD. Increased
  research proposal of 670 words to 9500 words. Identified and organised themes. Integrated personal component of rationale for the study.
  Wrote two case studies for research proposal. Made a lot of thinking
  links – a lot clearer.
- Started journal article from scratch (5200 words).
- Wrote first draft of findings chapter of PhD thesis, target 12,000 words,
  wrote 3000 words. Answered the two research questions I set out to
  answer and constructed tables, which is important for other chapters.
- Wrote 4000-word conference paper, toward journal article. Discussed
  and clarified the conceptual framework with colleague at retreat.
- Completed first draft of report on PhD, ready to hand in. Also generated
  ideas for the literature review and critique (3400 words). More importantly, started writing again. Wish I had done this even a few months ago,
  as I've been sitting worrying about my writing. Recognise now that writing goes through several stages. Will use this structure in my own time.
- Drafted literature review of PhD (9800 words). Clarity of thought and
  starting to make links. Discussion with colleague about this very important. Space to think about the research deeply enough is part of the effect.
- Wrote second draft of journal article (7000 now 10,900 words), a better
  draft, clearer, more coherent, and worked on all parts of it, i.e. edited
  all sections.

This list clearly illustrates productivity in a range of projects. Demonstrating productivity is an important component of social writing, not only for demonstrating
that it works, but also for defining exactly what participants' outputs are.

If it seems naïve to see numbers of words written and numbers of hours spent
writing as indicators of productivity, it should be noted – and we often discuss
this – that thinking and talking about writing in terms of specific tasks and sub-
tasks is how we do many other professional tasks, like marking, teaching and
research.

The process of working towards these outputs will have been the subject of several discussions in the course of the retreat, and this develops their and our understanding of what exactly that process is. What are the increments in writing a literature review of 9800 words? Of course there will be more than one way of defining these increments, but how useful it is to have it defined in specific terms, in terms of specific numbers of words – at each stage – and the amount of time required to write them – for each stage.

How useful would it be to discuss writing in these terms with doctoral students? How useful would they find it? How useful would it be for supervisors, students and researchers to reflect back on this process and think about how they produced this text: what the stages were, what role discussion played in developing thinking and writing, and what the increments were in producing this text. Otherwise, how would we know?

At this point, someone usually raises the 'quality question'. I have written about this before, but I cannot *not* write about it here, for fear of giving the impression that I think that any writing is good writing or that more words are better than fewer words. My point is that writing – like other research tasks – can be defined and discussed in terms of sub-tasks, and if people want to find time and space for writing, perhaps defining achievable sub-tasks will help. We can all agree that any text we produce will require review and revision, usually multiple revisions, before we can use the word 'quality', although perhaps we should define 'quality' itself: which qualities should a first draft have? What about a second draft? What about the final draft?

Community of Practice theory

We can use Community of Practice theory (Lave and Wenger 1991) to explain how structured writing retreat works (Murray and Newton 2009), using three components:

- mutuality of engagement – engaging with and responding to other writers and giving and receiving feedback on writing-in-progress;
- identity of participation – building on mutual engagement to develop an identity as a writer; and
- legitimate peripheral participation – experiencing the legitimacy of writing and legitimising the self as writer.

Structured writing retreats provide an 'approximation of full participation that gives exposure to actual practice' (Wenger 1998: 100). For some, this is the only experience of participation that is available. However, being at a retreat means being both a part of and apart from a community of writing practice, and this may mean developing the skill of negotiating that paradox.

This analysis argues that at a retreat participants can learn through participation; it may be much more difficult, even impossible, to learn without this – or some other form of – participation. While participants already 'knew how to write', at structured writing retreats they learn new practices, and they learn that the key mechanism of this is the presence of and interactions with other writers. They do not learn this because I tell them this is what they will get from retreats; this is what participants tell me they get from retreats.

Where we may feel that we have to part company with Wenger's model is with the idea of 'apprenticeship'. Academics and professionals are perhaps less likely to feel that they are 'apprentices' in writing, a word they are more likely to associate with doctoral students. However, at retreats people regularly report that they are still learning to write: 'One or two retreats aren't going to have a miraculous huge change in practice . . . these kinds of changes are gradual' (Murray and Newton 2009: 552).

Outcomes

In addition to significant outputs on the way to publication and completion, structured writing retreats produce other outcomes. The following are representative comments from five retreats held in 2013:

- Writing in new ways

  o Strange at first to be told to sit down and write, but after the first few minutes it seemed really natural.
  o The structure makes you press on with difficult writing.
  o Good to explore it for different types of writing – different objectives you can still achieve in the two days. Explores the breadth/depth of your writing. Comparing getting lots of words on paper with other ways of writing.

- Dedicating time to writing

  o Good structure . . . to have dedicated writing time and dedicated breaks. Keeps you motivated. Preparation is key – I always feel I'm more productive here where I've prepared thoroughly. Planning what work you're going to do here – giving it about a day, after having done the reading.
  o Crucial to have time dedicated to writing. Also retreats work as targets – as prompt to prepare for writing at retreats.
  o Good to develop ways to unplug from technology in order to write.

- Structuring the writing day

  o . . . having to sit down for a fixed amount of time was very useful. Several times I had the urge to stop because I got to a difficult bit, which I would do at home. But I thought I might as well get on with it, which made me get over the difficult bit. I find that really useful. With practice you probably get better at that. Sticking to time limits – when writing at home – will be really important.

o   Earlier writing seems more like freewriting, but over the day links emerge. Starting to make links between ideas.

o   Useful to quantify the writing tasks, sub-tasks and sub-sub-tasks – makes you think about what you really have to do, think about and decide on the emphasis in the argument etc. Again, you can apply a specific amount of time to specific number of words. Makes it feel more achievable.

o   The whole process of stopping and taking a break is part of the effect. It's a healthy process.

•   Legitimising writing as part of our job

o   It seems strange that writing is such a big part of our job, but it never gets privileged in our workplace. There are always interruptions, but there are no interruptions here

o   There is a concentration that develops when we are all writing together that helps you to sustain your writing, even though we are all working on different things. Develops a good feeling – all striving away together. It stops me doing six things at a time, which is what I normally do. You quickly lose your train of thought. Or you just scan what you're reading – here you can concentrate. When you're in the office you want to read – but it almost seems like wasted time because you're not producing anything. There is also overload at work; here you can focus on a piece of work and make progress.

o   We are expected to be there, at work – that is part of the problem. There is a guilt that comes with writing – you should be doing other things, but writing is part of your job.

•   Building writing- and research-oriented relationships

o   I wasn't sure what I was coming to, even having read the article about retreat [Murray and Newton 2009]. There was anxiety about the writing and the set up and my ability, but I am going away more confident. We all have the same anxieties – good to see that others are in the same boat.

o   Because we are on [different] campuses, this is a good opportunity to meet colleagues. Now joined each other's networks. Finding opportunities for doing research together.

o   Making connections here – and taking connections back to campus – to keep writing going.

o   We got to see each other outside the professional context – good for breaking down barriers. Bridging and bonding – social capital – this underpins work we do – working relationships enhanced.

o   Good to network with other people, see different levels people are at, share information. It's assumed we know all this, but we learned a lot.

o   Healthy cross-faculty, cross-disciplinary discussions that happen here, but don't happen so much on campus.

These outcomes show that it's not just about the writing. Writing is connected to everything else. This linkage is clearest among returners and 'serial attenders' at these retreats. They tend to make more space for reading and focus their reading towards specific writing projects. On the basis of this evidence of impact, should a writing retreat be a one-off? Or will regular attendance at retreats embed these benefits in our work?

Putting writing retreats in research strategy

Where does writing sit in the work of an institution? How does it relate to strategy and other ways of working? If there are no interactions about writing in the workplace, what can an individual do about that? If such interactions are likely to be stigmatised – rather than seen as intellectual exchange – who would choose to engage in them? Where would they take place? When? There are no established norms or principles on which to draw for answers to these questions.

Does this mean that it is up to individuals to form groupings in which they can discuss their writing, even if these groupings are not in their workplaces? How feasible will that be? How practical is that? Can people who met at a retreat, for example, easily continue to meet in other groupings to sustain the impact of this way of writing? Is the answer to institutionalise retreats – to make them part of institutional strategy?

In most cases, retreats are funded by institutions, but usually not on a long-term, ongoing basis, with some exceptions: one department made writing retreats part of its research strategy and held two retreats every year, and people could attend as many retreats as they wanted. As a way of supporting research, this was praised by the External Examiner, which, in turn, validated the strategy.

Arguments can, therefore, be made for embedding retreats in a research strategy:

1   Making progress with research

- Research 'epiphanies' – step changes and turning points in research thinking.
- Quality of concentration – clear thinking and problem solving.
- Working through challenging points in research, especially in relation to research design and methodology.
- Increased research productivity, measured in terms of thinking, writing and ongoing research activity after retreats.

2   Importance of structure for research

- Develops persistence and resilience in dealing with problems in research.
- Instils pacing in research activity and, thereby, the capacity for sustaining research activity after retreats.

3   The research peer group effect

- Develops collegiality in research – 'we're all in the same boat'.
- Fosters sharing of research methods, concepts and references.
- Develops and sustains research collaborations and networks.
- Leads to connections between research-active colleagues from different institutions/departments/campuses and different disciplines.
- Boosts participants' confidence in their research activities, particularly important for early career researchers, doctoral students and staff on masters or doctoral courses.
- Celebrates research achievements, e.g. publications, PhD completions.

The argument is that the outputs and outcomes of structured writing retreats are features of a research culture. This form of retreat can be a mechanism for developing research cultures. If retreats are not part of research strategies, what are they? How will they be funded (after an initial trial)? Participants often fund them out of their own pockets, but should they have to do so? Not everyone can afford that. Isn't that putting the onus back on individuals?

Extending the model: micro-groups

> A shiny new community can spring up overnight miles from anywhere, then fade away just as fast.
>
> (Packer 2013: 4)

Earlier studies showed that it was difficult and often impossible to transfer the skills and strategies developed at retreat to workplace settings (Murray and Cunningham 2011). Some strategies travelled back from retreat and were sustained for a short period, but not over the long term. This mirrors other findings, discussed in earlier chapters, that there are limitations to the long-term impact of many interventions designed to develop writing activity.

However, recently it has become clear that retreat participants have found ways to transfer the structured retreat model to a range of times and spaces (Murray 2014) by meeting in small groups of two to five people. These micro-groups are easy to organise, have small numbers, more flexibility, can be more regular, non-residential, in a range of timeslots and spaces, but always with the same people. This means people who buy into the social writing model, particularly those who have attended structured writing retreat:

> I found that writing groups were an extension of the practices from writing retreat. This helped me to continue with writing all year round so I did not

see retreats as isolated events . . . writing groups bring continuity and discipline . . . so you keep going with the writing even when you can't see the light at the end of the tunnel.

More specifically, these micro-groups replicate the structured writing retreat programme:

I used the organised writer's retreats to write up my entire doctoral thesis. During a period of 18 months I attended nine of these 2 and ½ day retreats. These took place at locations commutable from Glasgow, however far enough away to prevent any distractions from home. The groups of students who attended these retreats were very varied, with none of them coming from the same background as myself . . . Off the back of these writer's retreats I got to know other writers who were keen to continue the retreat structure back home. I met up with 1 other writer on approximately 4 occasions outwith the organised retreats to do more structured writing. On one occasion we met in a coffee shop. We kept to the retreat timetable.

Alternatively, they adapt the structured retreat programme. Different groups can meet at different times, for different periods and in different places. For example, one person listed five types of micro-group meeting that he attended:

I have written in groups in a range of settings:

- I have attended formal writing retreats of between 8 and 14 people writing for 10 hours across 2 days with a preparation evening beforehand.
- Writing groups in my academic department, meeting occasionally on a pre-planned basis to write for a half- or full day.
- Writing days at colleagues' houses, again writing for around 5 hours.
- Paired-writing sessions for pre-determined times, writing in a room in a colleague's department.
- Coffee shop sessions meeting for 60–90 minutes at the beginning of a day.

Writing in these groups, participants find, protects writing from distractions and makes it easier to achieve clarity of thought. This then becomes the purpose of such meetings:

The structure of the group acts as a physical barrier to distractions. Sticking with the writing process, not being distracted, not checking emails, not looking up references on the internet are all part of the process of writing in a group. As a result, because the threats of disengagement with writing are largely removed, the writer is only left with their writing, and even though it is sometimes difficult, by sticking with and staying with the writing process, epistemological clarity does emerge.

This legitimises writing and writers. It also legitimises social writing:

> you feel as though you and those around you are engaged in the same endeavour. This makes it a bit easier to feel as though what you are doing has meaning and is mutually beneficial . . . the sense that this is the right thing to be doing at this time in the company of these particular people. The shared practice gives it a kind of legitimacy.

That these groups foster a sense of collectivity is clear from the terms participants use to describe them – 'common experience', 'collective discipline', 'like-mindedness', 'camaraderie', 'writing relationship', 'positive pressure . . . positive competition' and 'fellowship'. These qualities are implicated in their developing focus on and persistence with their writing. As are qualities they recognise in each other, which they see as constructing this collectivity: empathy, trust and mutual respect. This is not, therefore, just about writing in a group, but about developing new norms for social writing:

> this isn't just sharing a space together (sharing an office or the like) it needs to be that both [writers] are engaged in the group writing ethos – because you create tacit rules and obligations – to show up, to keep to time, to make good use of the time, to be supportive. These norms are powerful and need to be enforced by the group leader or in established groups by the group itself. These keep it as a special time and form of writing. You can't let too much chat creep in or it becomes another time thief.

While this seems like common sense – if you set aside time to write with others, and if you make each other stick to that time, then you will surely write – but in most professional and academic settings this is not common practice. This may partly explain why writing remains problematic in those settings.

The key point is that those who write in micro-groups say that it is not where they write but who they write with that matters. The physical space and timing of their writing sessions are less important than writing with others who commit to writing in structured sessions. This is social writing in the sense that, for the structure to work, the presence of other writers is important to maintain the structure, along with brief discussions about writing. The presence of other people is a factor in writing.

For many, the social writing effect is much stronger, much more productive than solitary writing. Their mutual agreement to write forms a kind of social contract. In some ways this functions as a community of practice, a 'social, situated practice' for writing (Aitchison and Lee 2006) and a supportive culture for writing (Clughen and Hardy 2012).

Can we, therefore, go as far as saying that it is not more time and space to write that we need as much as more relationships formed around the act of writing? Is it that these relationships create capacity to make time and space for writing? Is that really a 'capacity', or is it a constructive response to the intensifying atomisation of work and life? And does it work to sustain writing in that context?

Conclusion: privileging writing or privileging writers?

Initially, when I started to run structured writing retreats and began to gather data about people's experiences of them, it seemed that these retreats created an idealised environment for writing, so that the return to the 'real world' of work and life often felt overwhelming – for me as much as for them.

Back then, my aim was simply to answer a plea for more time and space to write. Over time, however, we all began to notice significant changes occurring when people wrote together in this way and, more importantly, when they talked about their writing-in-progress in this way. Instead of the much-feared dependency of the 'needy', what seemed to be happening was the conscious management of writing by the productive. It was not that they 'needed' retreats to write, but that they used strategies learned at retreats to manage and sustain their writing.

> I am never as productive working alone.

We now know that it would be wrong to see this statement as a sign of weakness or lack of motivation. The person who said this is a highly productive 'serial attender' at structured writing retreats and micro-groups, with a track record of publishing in high quality journals. This statement should, instead, be read as an indicator of the power of social writing.

The benefit of social writing should itself be the subject of discussion, of course, but as long as writing – the act of writing – is not discussed in the workplace, the frame of reference for any discussion is inevitably personalised and may be stigmatised. This makes it difficult to articulate a personal theory of writing or personal writing practices. Where there is no such articulation there may be little or no reflection, sharing and re-engineering of writing processes in the ways that seem to happen so routinely, so regularly and so comfortably at structured writing retreats.

In this context, these retreats provide a forum for developing the theory and practice of academic writing, while producing outputs. They allow individuals, working together, to develop their own social writing theory and practice, as evidenced by the growing number and variety of self-starting, self-directed, flexible micro-groups in so many places.

It is worth thinking about whether participation in these retreats requires some form of preparation for this way of working and/or the formal instruction in rhetoric covered in earlier chapters. But most people, once they start writing at retreats, realise that they can write, that they can develop in writing by writing. People often realise that they were more prepared to write than they thought they were, and that they already have many skills and strategies for writing and subjects they want to write about.

A structured writing retreat allows them to bring these into play. This is, then, still about recruiting the benefits of writing in groups, but also about learning to set boundaries around writing, in terms of time and place, but with all the associated boundaries of argument, content, depth and self-expression that are invoked in discussions of writing 'time' and 'space'.

But how does this fit 'the system'? Removing ourselves from normal working environments to write – even for short periods in micro-groups in a café near work – is that always feasible? Is it sustainable? Will the arguments about outputs and outcomes generated by retreats – summarised above – be sufficient to legitimise doing writing and research in this way? Will 'the system' question the need for continuous funding for retreats – modest as it is – even when there are significant written outputs that directly or indirectly bring in research funding? Is there a risk in moving writing – and associated research activities and relationships – away from workplaces? Will someone begin to resent the relationships constructed at retreats? Will some feel excluded? Will some, in fact, be excluded?

Will scepticism and even valid criticism undermine writers' confidence? Could perceptions of participation in repeat-retreat affect promotion? Will concerns about any of these issues prevent retreat participants from talking about writing – or retreats – in their workplaces?

There is a risk that opening up writing to discussion in retreats and groups will, ironically, lead people to keep writing activities secret and/or selective. For example, one respondent in my study of micro-groups described selectivity around writing groups and secrecy around writing:

> I have asked one or two people to join us [to write in a micro-group] but for various reasons they haven't . . . I am very picky about who I ask though, and even really nice people whose work I respect can be quite critical about this as an idea for reasons below:
>
> 2 *How do you describe what you do to other people who are not in writing groups?*
>
> I pretty much don't. It's like a secret activity. Am trying to think why. Maybe because: in the past, when I have mentioned this it invites grief e.g. 'Oh well, it's ok for you. Lucky you, to find time to do this. Your workload/life must be so much easier than mine. I haven't got time to do this. I am completely swamped, overwhelmed with my huge teaching load and all the marking I have to do, so how come you have this time? Etc., etc. . . . '. This is of course nonsense. In my Dept I have seen the REF [UK Research Excellence Framework] submissions, and with one or two exceptions everyone has done really well. So they are all finding time to write, and we are all pretty busy. But nevertheless, there always seems to be a bit of resentment that I am doing this. And a sense that I could or should be doing something else. I don't like the hassle, and I don't want my writing time threatened by others who might wish to see me do other things. So I just keep my head down and quietly get on with it. Have, as noted above, occasionally asked colleagues

if they want to join me and usually they say no. And I often get a sense of disapproval even if this is not stated.

No one else in my Dept talks about writing practices. They all present themselves as over pressured and far too busy to write. As noted above this can't be the case as they are all publishing. But writing practice is denied and not shared.

This respondent and her colleagues are all producing writing, but this culture does not exactly facilitate social writing, and social writing is unlikely to work for all of them. Nor would those who are successfully writing, but denying it, be remotely interested in social writing. Hence the connection between their denial and her selectivity?

To emphasise how common this view is, here is a comment from one of the people who read a draft of this chapter:

One of my PhD supervisors originally made disparaging comments about retreats but now accepts that this is a legitimate way forward for some. I'm still working on getting her to understand that it's a way forward for many.

However, many PhD students would not have the confidence or stamina to persist in trying to persuade a sceptic, and these 'disparaging comments' will prevent many students from talking about the benefits of writing in this way.

This is a familiar theme when we talk about writing: there are people in a range of professions who feel they have to 'sneak writing in' to their workplaces and 'not advertise the fact that [they are] writing' (Murray and Newton 2008: 31). There are potentially serious consequences for early career researchers and others of keeping writing – the act of writing – secret. Is this about secrecy surrounding writing in institutions, rather than a new level of secrecy about what goes on at retreats and in micro-groups?

What if an institution demands closer surveillance of retreats? What would that mean? How would that affect participation? How would it affect perceptions of what goes on at retreats? Should we invest more time and energy in getting the system to value these retreats, or would that just distract us from our writing?

What if our managers decide that they want to know how we spend every hour at retreat or micro-group? It is established practice in many workplaces to fill in a calendar to show what we do hour by hour. Would that affect the process? Would it affect our outputs and outcomes? Would it affect participation? Would it affect repeat participation? Should we invite managers to participate in a retreat? (They usually decline the invitation, with the one exception of the department described above that made retreats part of research strategy.) Why do managers not attend in the same numbers? Why do more women than men usually attend?

A culture of surveillance will create the imperative of careful reporting of outcomes and outputs – not a bad thing in itself, for reasons discussed in the next chapter – so as to protect retreats from potential attack by the system. But in doing this are we practising self-surveillance? How can we develop self-regulation in a way that does not simply provide information for the system but also helps us add to knowledge, in terms of both our own knowledge – of our research and of writing – and the knowledge base in our field?

Structured writing retreat is a mode of social writing, so that writing – and research – is no longer an exclusively solitary activity. It establishes relationships among those who want to write in competitive times. It provides a place for resistance and dissent in performative settings. It resists surveillance. It allows connectivity and cohesion to develop around writing.

For these reasons it is both nurturing and risky. For all it feels like a safe environment, some will see it as risky, even dangerous. A place that provides a space for dissent can be seen as a threat. What happens when management find out that there are dissenting conversations at retreats? How would they react if they found out that conversations that cannot take place at work – particularly in open-plan offices – were happening at retreats?

What if writing retreat participants come to be seen as privileged? How will those who choose not to attend feel? What about those who cannot afford to attend? People with caring responsibilities? People with children? People who are fearful that retreat is just another competition? Could writing retreat accentuate existing divisions between those who write and those who do not? Could it be seen as discriminatory? Is it discriminatory? Does it perpetuate other forms of discrimination, or could it be used to that end?

To conclude, in the competitive writing culture that predominates, structured writing retreats produce cohesion in competitive cultures, create structure out of the fragments of time available for writing and build connectedness through the articulation of common goals, struggles and experiences.

The components of social writing used in structured writing retreats are:

- a structure that participants commit to and adapt after retreats;
- a series of conversations about writing-in-progress for specific projects; and
- a shared recognition that talking about writing is doing research.

This is not, of course, the whole story. Given that retreats are not available to everyone, and that most of those who attend are not able to do so as often as they would like, and certainly not regularly, we need to think about other forms of social writing that will sustain productivity and creativity – that will sustain writing, for those who want to write. This means confronting the concept of performativity and working out how to construct our productivity in a range of settings – that is, a range of *our* settings.

This is not about forcing collectives, but about creating an environment where people can create them, but we have to acknowledge that structured writing retreats will not necessarily protect everyone from the side effects of performativity, a problem addressed in the next chapter.

Chapter 6

Productivity

It is the time to ask what scholarship is about and – I strongly suggest – to change our standards. What we have is a system with little or no room for individual agency

I have the strongest sensation that many of the people who have the most to say are most reluctant to say it. And I think the academy should enlist publishers to try to get some of the silent people to talk. Forget the blabbermouths. They will find their way.

I think our present mania for publication is a great insult to the dignity of thought, the dignity upon which the authority society might bestow on us is based. Deep thought does not always announce itself in shouts, but sometimes in whispers.

(Waters 2004: 16, 20, 21)

When writing is closely scrutinised – primarily in terms of outputs – there can be ambivalence about the explicit and implicit demands of a system that is designed to regulate our writing.

In this system, we have to decide if we want to write to make a difference, to add to knowledge and/or have an impact in the so-called real world? Or do we want to have an impact in terms of scoring points by publishing in a specific journal? Or do we want to do both? Will we attend to the system and its surveillance and/or to our own ideas and our sense of audiences? How will we do this?

It would be over-simplistic to attribute this ambivalence towards externally imposed writing targets to naïvety and to dismiss it as the growing pains of the developing writer, when many experienced and eminent writers feel the same way (Carnell *et al.* 2008). Nor should we see this ambivalence as reluctance or inability to write, since that too oversimplifies the act of writing in a surveillance culture.

This culture may not provide a forum for safely and routinely discussing these issues, and yet, if they are not resolved, they can impinge on motivation to write and may thereby inhibit the development of writing and writers. How people work through these issues – often, presumably, on their own – is not known. In any case, the demands on writers and directives on writing often seem non-negotiable and highly politicised, and the criteria of 'publishability' seem no more neutral. There seems to be little room for individual choice or agency: 'Staff are encouraged to engage in research not on their own terms, but in the terms created by the department and by extension to the national funding and evaluation exercises' (Lucas 2009: 78).

In this context, the act of writing can be even more 'secret', as illustrated in Chapter 5, so that the process of producing measurable outputs is not exposed to scrutiny – which may be a good thing – but neither is it exposed to reflection. How we negotiate this context is never fully open to view. How we make it meaningful to ourselves is never really up for discussion. Some say it feels like they – as much as their writing – are the 'units' of assessment in this culture.

However, if we are going to write publicly, we need to have ways to negotiate this performative culture. We may need to align our writing goals with those of whatever research assessment system applies to our context or, more specifically, the goals of the institution where we work. If this sounds like assimilation into the collective – or if it feels like it – then we will have to do some work on our motivation. This means focusing on our motivation to write explicitly. Otherwise, not thinking about and planning ways to sustain our motivation may inhibit our writing.

The worst case scenario is that this culture will limit the development of social writing: a performative culture that fosters the 'commodification of knowledge' can affect relationships, creating, 'fundamental changes in the relationships between the learner, learning and knowledge . . . Knowledge and knowledge relations, including the relationships between learners, are de-socialized' (Ball 2003: 226). Such processes have a powerful impact on what counts as knowledge and can shape academic work and identity.

In this context Hey (2001: 40) proposes 'more collaborative ways of working' and encourages academics and researchers to savour the 'pleasure of resisting the individualistic ethos of higher education by persisting in collaborative work'. This chapter explores one way of developing such collaborative work by focusing on the practice of goal setting for writing, to be used in the context of groups of people who want to write. It elaborates on the argument developed in the previous chapter that the process of setting and monitoring goals is central to the impact of social writing and important for making progress with specific writing projects and/or the larger 'project' of finding ways to write more regularly or to write more about what we want to say.

This chapter describes a move from performativity to peer-formativity, by building peer relationships that promote writing in performative systems and by writing in ways that align with performative and other values, including, above all, our own.

The main argument of this chapter is that we can think about our writing as a behaviour – just like any other activity we do. This means that we can use the strategies for generating text covered in earlier chapters to define writing goals. We can thereby connect freewriting, writing to prompts and outlining to the development of self-efficacy in our writing. This may involve changing our writing behaviours by deliberately engaging in a process of behaviour change. Since sustainable behaviour change depends on social support, social writing has an important role to play.

Key messages

- We need to close the gap between externally imposed targets and personal values – we can use writing meetings to do this.
- Writing can be defined and conceptualised as a behaviour.
- Becoming a productive writer may involve behaviour change.
- Attempts to change writing behaviours benefit from social support.
- Discussing writing goals and progress is part of writing.

This chapter identifies some of the psychological processes involved in writing and shows how we can use them to facilitate our writing. It shows how we can make performativity the subject of discussion and reflection, and it provides strategies for negotiating performativity through mutual peer discussion of writing behaviours and goals. This follows on from the previous chapter – which argued for the importance of goals – by providing more specific examples and more detailed discussion of goal setting for writing.

Writing is a behaviour

> We are unsure of what aspects of work are valued and how to prioritize efforts. We become uncertain about the reasons for actions. Are we doing this because it is important, because we believe in it, because it is worthwhile? Or is it being done ultimately because it will be measured or compared? . . . much of this reflexivity is internalized. These things become matters of self-doubt and personal anxiety rather than public debate.
>
> (Ball 2003: 220)

How can you reduce writing to a set of behaviours? Surely it is more complex than that? Surely it is about intellectual acuity and having good data, or having something important and novel to write about? Is defining writing as a behaviour just another tool of performativity? Will it lead to micro-managing everyone's writing, and isn't that the purpose? Yes, micro-management is on the rise, but seeing writing as a behaviour is one way of deconstructing what it involves and reconstructing a process that works.

This may involve behaviour change, and there are ways to construct and adopt productive writing behaviours. However, even when we want to change our behaviours, even when that is a conscious intention or goal, there can still be ambivalence. What seems to be important is to address this ambivalence explicitly, rather than seeing it as legitimate resistance to external controls, for example. Choosing not to address it may limit motivation to write or, more likely, may produce conflicting motivations towards writing:

> The decisional conflict can result in . . . [people] being stuck in a state in which they are unable to change despite there being incentives to do so, or to alternate between engaging in a new behaviour pattern and relapsing to old behaviours.
>
> (Markland *et al*. 2005: 813)

This may be one way of revising what is often seen as the 'excuse' that there is no time to write; instead, it may be that there is decisional conflict about whether to write or not, an interpretation explored further in this chapter.

Behaviour change models may be more suited to writing than you think, particularly the motivational interview (Miller and Rollnick 2002). This incorporates individual values, motivation and social support in a change process. While previous chapters addressed these topics, this chapter introduces a way of changing our writing behaviours.

The motivational interview has been widely used, particularly, though not exclusively, in health promotion settings, where it is employed, for example, to support smoking cessation or raise physical activity levels (Loughlan and Mutrie 1995). In motivational interviews participants use goal setting, decisional balance – weighing the pros and cons of different courses of action they might take – anticipate barriers to proposed changes and use social support to achieve behaviour change.

There is ample evidence that this approach helps people achieve the goals they want to achieve but have difficulty achieving (Hughes *et al*. 2002, 2007; Kirk *et al*. 2009, 2010). Motivational interviewing can help to integrate intended and existing behaviours. Where this can make an important contribution to writing in performative settings is that it provides a mechanism for aligning a new goal – which might be extrinsic and/or intrinsic – with our own values. What makes it different from many other discussions of behaviour change – and perhaps from other discussions of writing – is that these are discussions between people who want to engage in a sympathetic exploration of barriers to a proposed change – such as making more time and space for writing – without wanting to impose change.

What is interesting about these discussions is that they not only expose but also raise awareness of discrepancies between our current behaviours and our goals and values. Above all, for behaviour change to be sustainable social support is key, which in this context occurs through interactions of various kinds.

If, in these conversations, we help each other to make our writing goals and sub-goals more specific, this will help us to think them through. Over time, we learn to set more realistic goals for the time that we actually have, and this lets us set boundaries between writing and our other goals – which often impinge on writing – and these discussions can help us focus on working towards these goals. Systems for assessing research in higher education and other contexts are likely to influence what, how and for whom people write (Murray 2014).

The literature on behaviour change shows that the more we achieve the goals we set ourselves, the more we develop the belief that we can achieve our goals (Bandura 1997). This is how self-efficacy develops. These concepts are rarely brought into discussions of writing (Boice 1990a). In fact, there is often concern that seeing writing this way will reduce it to a set of targets for the system to measure. I think the key is that this approach helps us to reduce our writing to a set of targets that *we* can measure, that we can take satisfaction in achieving and that we can also present for other measurement systems.

Moreover, choosing not to set writing goals and not to monitor progress in writing may lead to the opposite of self-efficacy. Yes, we know what we have to do, and yes, we know how to write, but if we do not set and monitor goals we are less likely to develop the belief that we can achieve our writing goals and will be less likely to achieve them.

Behaviour change theory may, therefore, offer an explanation for the recurring problem of making time to write, which seems to be a problem at every turn in the writing process and is therefore a topic addressed in every chapter of this book: it may not solely be about poor time management as much as about the need to develop the ability to define writing in terms of specific increments of time.

Writing meetings

This section describes an approach for putting this behaviour change theory into practice in relation to writing, the writing meeting. This form of meeting was adapted from other forms of motivational interview designed to promote behaviour change. It provides a framework for writers to negotiate externally imposed writing targets or standards and to work on intrinsic motivation and change writing behaviours. This can help those who are not writing to get started. It can help those who are writing to write more or with less stress and more confidence (i.e. confidence that they can write). The key to the effectiveness of this approach, as explained above, is social support. Without that, attempts to change behaviour are more likely to fail.

In writing meetings participants work in pairs, taking turns to act as (a) prompter, asking questions to prompt discussion of writing goals and plans and (b) writer, reporting on their own writing goals and experiences. The role of prompter includes writing down the writer's answers, which lets the writer focus on their answers to the questions.

These conversations involve six steps, as outlined in the Writing Meeting Template (see Appendix G), which is used to structure these meetings. The prompter uses this template to lead the writer through the six steps and notes the writer's responses on the template.

The first step in this discussion involves the prompter asking the writer to define where he or she is in the process of becoming a productive writer: 'contemplation', 'preparation', 'action' or 'maintenance'. 'Contemplation' means having the desire and/or intention to write; 'preparation' means currently not writing; 'action' means starting to write (for less than six months); and 'maintenance' means regularly writing (for six months or more).

The second step involves producing a 'decisional balance', in which the prompter asks the writer to list the benefits of writing and the drawbacks of not writing and writes these down.

In the third step the writer defines barriers to writing and explores ways of overcoming them.

For the fourth step the prompter asks the writer to set writing goals.

The fifth involves prompting the writer to anticipate barriers to achieving these goals.

The sixth step involves prompting the writer to define actions he or she will take to achieve these goals.

The writer then takes on the role of the prompter and vice versa.

The following quotation and others in this section are from a study of writing meetings funded by the Nuffield Foundation (Murray and Thow forthcoming). They are from transcripts of interviews with fourteen people who used the writing meetings over a period of eight weeks, meeting every two weeks and spending, on average, an hour in each meeting.

> It was very, very helpful to identify what the pros and cons [of writing] were . . . benefits in the first week far outweighed the negative aspects, but it was really just to clarify our thinking and subsequent understanding of what it is, and the 'whys'.

In many settings, discussions of writing do not usually include personal values and beliefs, but are more likely to focus on institutional 'whys' and external targets and rankings. The definition of what writing 'counts' in any sense, while seemingly transparent, can be complex, malleable and unstable, shaped by competing definitions of quality and impact. Those who want to write recognise the complexity of rating new knowledge and new writing and understand the difficulty of creating fixed definitions of quality writing. Yet, this fluidity can be destabilising and even demotivating.

In this context, the decisional balance section of this conversation is a space not only to consider external forces that influence our writing but also to bring our values into this discussion. This works as an 'outlet for discussion on the position of writing', as one participant in this study put it. This suggests that we can use writing meetings to construct a position for writing. This, in turn, can increase our motivation to write and could facilitate the privileging of writing and, as one participant put it, 'strengthen our values and beliefs about writing'.

More specifically, in this study the benefits of writing and the drawbacks of not writing were articulated in personal – not just performative – terms, as in the following examples from all the writers' templates filled in during meetings in this study:

- What are the benefits of writing?
    o   Distils thoughts and ideas.
    o   Forms possible direction and purpose.
    o   It surprises.
    o   Continue to extend own writing skills.
    o   Making professional links with colleagues to further my own practice.
    o   Extending professional knowledge and partnerships in and outside university.
    o   Remaining current in practice and connected to professional expectations.
    o   Clarifies thinking.
    o   Reflect.
    o   Sense of accomplishment.
    o   Pulls you into new ideas and themes to explore by engaging with literature.
    o   Lifts confidence and affirms work in the field.
    o   Status.
    o   Feeding ideas back into teaching.

By contrast, the drawbacks of not writing were often associated with external signs or recognition of failure and punishment, often internalised as 'guilt':

- What are the drawbacks of not writing?
    o   Not fulfilling professional expectations.
    o   Questions about my commitment to my area in the university.
    o   Not meeting university targets.
    o   Not meeting external requirements.
    o   Pressure of not fulfilling professional expectations.
    o   Big pressure when not writing – feel the expectation to publish.
    o   Feeling guilty, unproductive and falling behind in my schedule.
    o   Procrastination – pressure this induces.
    o   Lose the thread.
    o   Lose touch with content and concepts.
    o   Takes up your thoughts even when not writing – can result in sleepless nights.
    o   Guilt when not writing, but also when writing and not doing other things.

However, there were some who saw it the other way round and inverted the template's questions – 'Well, actually there are some drawbacks in writing, and benefits in not writing':

- What are the benefits of not writing?
  - o Letting your mind 'play with' ideas – the need for thinking time.
  - o Having space to be creative, to think about ideas and make connections.
  - o Time to do other things.
  - o Sometimes need down time, time away.
  - o Need time for reading.
  - o Having time for things to incubate, let thoughts and ideas come to the surface.
  - o Having time for self and family.

These are not excuses for not writing as much as a longing for activities that foster writing, although many said that they saw drawbacks in writing:

- What are the drawbacks of writing?
  - o It can be stressful – the actual writing process.
  - o No institutional support.
  - o Focus on detail takes mind away from 'big picture'.
  - o Submitting for peer review and coping with negative reviews.
  - o Writing is hard work – have to learn how.
  - o Brain turning to mush – just too much going on.
  - o Bogged down in data – hard to concentrate with possibilities data throws up.

The counterpoint of terms related to ideas of 'play' and 'bogged down' in this list suggests a tension between desire to engage with writing and fear of being overwhelmed by it:

> I very often didn't meet my [writing] targets . . . What we'd tried to do was think what we'd do in the next fortnight before we met each other again. So we both had long-term goals, which shifted about a little bit because we added to them, I think [small laugh]. So it was, 'Yes, I think that would be manageable within a fortnight, but there may be things get in the way', and in fact . . . I kept setting the same short-term goal and then began to think, 'Well, is this what I really should be doing in this time?'

This individual took this opportunity to interrogate the imperative for writing articles in journals that 'count' in some form of assessment process: 'I'm having to work out myself how far I'm prepared to go with that. . . . I'm just churning out stuff for the sake of it and I don't particularly want to do that'. This is an excellent example of ambivalence about writing: this is a productive writer, with ample knowledge of writing and publications in several genres who is reluctant to write for – in fact, because of – external targets. This shows how the writing meeting can allow for this kind of negotiation with systems for evaluating writing. The writing meeting is a space for legitimising this negotiation:

I think going through this exercise actually helps, because one of the things we did do as well, was talk about the positions academics find themselves in with respect to this kind of task. . . . why you write and how far you're prepared to go with other people's purposes and how far with your own.

At these writing meetings it was/is, therefore, possible to acknowledge and begin to work through ambivalence towards writing.

Once writing goals are set, the next step is anticipating barriers to writing and identifying times when writing plans, could be 'at risk'. This part of the conversations prompted thinking about avoiding (rather than overcoming) barriers to writing:

With regard to defining time within the week that would be protected for writing . . . my [writing meeting] partner and myself found that removing ourselves from the university building was the best way of achieving that, because, again, the problems or barriers to writing tended to be if you're present . . . and students . . . you get caught up and deflected. Whereas, if you have time at home – and this would be depending on the individual – but I've certainly found that if I allocate that, it then becomes a behaviour.

These meetings led to change in the writing behaviours of participants in this study. Their conversations revealed changes in each other's writing behaviours during the study:

One of the things that seemed to become really clear to me over the three times that we did [the writing meeting] was that [my writing meeting partner] was getting better at making realistic goals or targets, given the other demands . . . Then being able to meet those goals put him just in a better place as well, and that has a knock-on effect.

Such changes were reinforced in these conversations, and writing achievements could be celebrated when, for example, articles were accepted. In these ways, these meetings created a peer-formative process, in the sense that they recruited peer support to enable academics and researchers to achieve their writing goals: 'Just telling your story [to someone]. . . . Just saying, "Well this is what I was doing", and as you spoke you started to think'.

Meeting other writers regularly to discuss writing can, therefore, be powerful on several levels: 'It was like having another conscience'; the meetings helped to 'share the guilt' and made writing less lonely; 'you know that the fears you have . . . you are not alone'. The potential effect is not simply to make writers feel better about writing; it can also develop thinking about writing and change writing behaviours: 'as you spoke you started to think'.

A key change in writing behaviour that can be achieved through writing meetings is the shift from external to internal attribution, the move from a position of relinquishing control to taking control of writing. This might mean moving from, 'the obvious [barriers] are the ones that we have very little control over. . . . it was things like, "We've got teaching to do," or, "We've got marking to do." And you know those things are just there' to taking control:

> The Decisional Balance conversation I think kind of crystallized in my mind that there's no reason not to [write] really. It . . . became quite stark that . . . if . . . I could think of all the reasons about how I feel bad if I'm not writing and how, you know, it's better to keep on top of it and all that kind of thing. So, having had that conversation, I think that just kind of made me think, well, just get on with it.

That this change can occur during a 'Decisional Balance conversation', emphasises the importance of peer discussion of writing and social support of this type. Using this peer component, writers can clarify what they want to write and explicitly connect their aspirations with external expectations:

> how we can navigate what our professional interests might be, and expertise might be, and link that to the priorities that the university has. And that again takes time. It takes time to think, and again for identifying groups that we'll be writing within, so that that writing group, or that research group has got an identity and we're not just lone academics [laughing, then in a posh accent], 'Oh, I think I'll write about this today'. There's a substance to it and a body to the writing. So . . . my beliefs in the importance of writing have been developed because I can understand that you are able, if you're persistent, to find a locus for writing that will provide some evidence of being able to meet the external expectations that are upon us as academics.

This reveals negotiations between institutional expectations and personal 'beliefs in the importance of writing', as they occur in writing meetings. This makes the case for a group and 'locus' for writing. These writing meetings can make this thinking possible, and they can be formative of writing and writers in the sense that they allow writers to articulate and mutually affirm the position of writing in their lives and to invoke their own values in that affirmation. However, acting on these intentions can still be problematic:

> I can't say I did it 100% consistently, but I did do it more actively in terms of explicitly putting [writing] into the diary, and maybe the symbolism of that is more powerful than one necessarily realises without thinking about it a little bit. But the things normally that go in my diary, and probably colleagues' diaries are, you know, what classes you're teaching, kind of thing, and that's legitimate, and that's hard and fast. Whereas, you know, these softer things actually need to go in there too, or they get edged out.

Such attempts to privilege writing on a regular basis can benefit from peer support of this type. These meetings can not only support discussions of writing but also address conflicts between writing and other roles and activities. In this way, such conflicts were not always sticking points.

However, in performative cultures these writing meetings can, ironically, be mistaken for monitoring:

> there are probably some academics who don't need this and others who may resist the explicit kind of structured nature of it, but I think for a lot of us who have our struggles, when we actually are honest about our struggles with writing, it's probably quite useful.

Writing meetings could be used as a mechanism of regulation or micromanagement. However, in purpose and effect they are the very opposite: their purpose is to enable academics and researchers to re-connect writing to their values, and their effect is to help them write in performative settings. In fact, in this way, 'writing goals' come to seem intrinsic rather than extrinsic:

> to engage in a more deliberate goal oriented way in order to accomplish and manage the pressure of having to accomplish, I think is really important. And so I kind of always believed that was important, but I think it strengthened that belief and the resolve to kind of act on that belief.

This 'deliberate goal oriented way' is not a mechanistic process of assimilation into performativity; this quotation suggests that writers – through writing meetings – can rediscover their desire to achieve their writing goals. This suggests a new level of commitment to 'not allow[ing] the slippage and the hi-jacking and all of that'. The role of peer discussions in achieving this was made quite explicit:

> I found it . . . quite therapeutic . . . this is why I think we've found it therapeutic: some of the guilt we could sort of help each other with and say, 'Yeh, well that was a reasonable thing to do', you know . . . so that was a good way of spending time.

This does not mean that writing meetings are 'therapeutic' in the sense that they provide comfort for conflicted writers; instead, they enable writers to engage with conflicts and move towards resolving them and, more importantly, to get into the habit of doing so:

> The first [writing meeting] took longer, and I think it should, because you're re-engaging with these things, and it's much more deeply reflective. Whereas the subsequent ones were quicker and probably should be, because you're . . . it's more maintenance of what . . . of the work you did and that supporting of goal setting and stuff . . . and then every so often having a lengthier one, to kind of re-connect and everything, would be good.

The underpinning theory of motivational interviews would predict that writing meetings will help writers align external drivers and internal goals, and that social support will be key to this effect. The positive impact of peer support for writing (Lee and Boud 2003) is well known; what is less well understood is the role of mutual peer discussions of writing as a way not only of privileging writing but of confronting and negotiating barriers to doing so. The writing meeting is a way of doing this.

Setting writing goals

> This turning of real lives into writing is no longer a procedure of heroization; it functions as a procedure of objectification and subjection.
>
> (Foucault 1977: 192)

This conveys the potential for objectifying and subjugating writing and writers that is a perceived risk in monitoring writing.

> We must cease once and for all to describe the effects of power in negative terms: it 'excludes', it 'represses', it 'censors', it 'abstracts', it 'masks', it 'conceals'. In fact, power produces; it produces reality; it produces domains of objects and rituals of truth. The individual and the knowledge that may be gained of him [sic] belong to this production.
>
> (Foucault 1977: 194)

This seems to encourage us to engage with power in order to play an active role. To do this in our 'real lives' may be difficult, but not impossible. To do so using social processes in the 'production' of writing is more likely to work. This section looks more closely at what writers do when they set writing goals. Using goal setting for writing should help in three ways:

1   helping to focus on the task;
2   developing confidence in the ability to perform the task; and
3   supporting the plan for achieving it, thus further increasing confidence in the ability to achieve writing goals.

Most people will know what their writing goals are, probably in quite specific terms: published outputs, doctoral completions, target journals and impact factors. What might be less defined is how the goal of writing a journal article may be broken down into sub-goals. This section analyses writers' goals with a view to shedding light on the use of goal setting for writing: what do specific goals, sub-goals and sub-sub-goals look like? How do these goals fit into specific increments of time?

A goal-setting template was developed for the structured writing retreats described in the previous chapter. Writers filled in templates at several points each day. In brief discussions they self-monitored and discussed their writing goals in pairs. When they discussed what they had written, they prompted each other to make their goals more specific, in terms of time slots they had for writing in the programme. This involved deciding how long a specific writing task would take, how many words it required and its purpose, scope and content. In these terms – numbers of words and minutes – writing goals can be specific and measurable. Without these numbers, goals are not specific.

At structured writing retreats, and at micro-group meetings after retreats, writers review their goals at the end of the morning, at the end of a writing session or at the end of the day. They can use their templates to review the extent to which they achieved their goals. This discussion allows for re-setting of goals that are not achieved.

This goal-setting template can be used not only to define goals, but also to prompt reflection on the setting of realistic writing goals. This was an important function of the template: if goal setting is potentially so important in writing, then we need a mechanism for articulating, sharing and reviewing writing goals. In discussion we can consider how specific, measurable and motivational our goals are, and what exactly the process of goal setting involves. We can compare records of writing goals and achievements, in order to gather insights into different ways of using goal setting for writing, using completed templates, such as the example in Table 6.1.

This is not to say that everyone will or should produce such detailed accounts of progress, but this process does show some of the workings of writing. For this writer, writing about her goals and monitoring progress towards them in this way and to this extent also did some of the thinking of writing and re-writing. It also shows the beginnings of further writing, for other articles.

This approach to goal setting for writing, using this template, can trigger many reactions. Some reject the very concept of goal setting for writing in these time periods and formats:

> Could not see how I would have long-term goals on a 2-day retreat.

> Confusing: progress under each one – how do you measure progress for your long-term goal?

Others absorb the concept of goal setting and immediately find it useful:

- 'Useful to have it'.
- 'Use it on every retreat – helped me clarify my goals'.
- 'Notes to self: in relation to progressing these goals'.
- 'Helped me to be a bit more organised'.
- 'Having it as a record, ticking things off – want to keep it as an audit trail'.
- 'Would be helpful if you were coming back again, it could act as a prompt'.
- 'Interesting looking at other people's'.

This suggests that, for some, the template itself is a useful device for managing – not just monitoring – their writing.

Goal-setting template

Day 1   **Day 2**

Goal   *Goal*

Long term

Progress

Medium term

Progress

Short term

Progress

Figure 6.1 Goal-setting template for self-monitoring and reflection

Table 6.1 Goal-setting template, completed

Time	Goal	Progress
9.30–11.00	Continue with paper: methodology. Revised goal/next step: work out shape of paper and how to "tell the story".	After a half hour or so faffing about and fiddling with syntax etc. I finally got my act together. I now have a shape and a structure, so at least I can work though that and see where it gets me. I've too many words and not enough references. Now I'm going to work through the section on findings from the 3 research questions. Next step: tighten and cut 3 research Q answers and add references.
11.30–12.30	Continue with paper: pedagogical model. Revised next step (in light of day 1): try to get to the writing of the next section. Revised, revised next step: tighten and cut 3 research Q answers, add references. Aim for about 2500 words.	OK, so all change, again. I decided that I'm trying to cram 2 ideas/themes into one paper and that's why it's not working. I've gone over the introduction and first sections and linked them in more closely with what is now the main section: the report of the overall findings of the research in terms of finding answers to the 3 research questions. This has taken just over 5000 words. The model just won't fit now and really needs another paper to do it justice. I think this might be for another journal, actually – or maybe a general journal. So, what I now want to do is finish the paper in under 1500 more words. I've come up with a heading. See what I'm getting at but probably can tighten it up a bit. This afternoon, for this last session, I want to get a handle on this last bit and round it all off with a clear message. That's my plan.
1.30–4.00	Continue with paper: model and practical application. Revised next step (in light of this morning): plan and try to put together next section and, perhaps, the conclusion.	Worked for another hour-and-a-half but got tied in knots. I need to refocus. What's the key message? If it's not about presenting the model, but outlining the findings of the research, what are my conclusions? How will they fit with the large middle section so that the whole thing seems cohesive? Questions for the next session. Meanwhile, for the last part of the afternoon (till about 5pm) I wrote 1000 words for Part 2 of the assignment essay, so the day wasn't wasted. This will need a re-write to make it more analytical, reflective and academic, but that's for later . . .

This idea that we can set out to produce measurable amounts of writing may sound simplistic, and the notion that we can develop productive writing behaviours may sound like we are all mere cogs in the publishing machine, churning out papers for the sake of it, rather than generating new knowledge or having any real impact.

However, if we discuss our writing goals with others who are writing and monitoring their goals, we will all articulate what those goals are, and this often changes things. Instead of having a general goal of submitting an article by the end next month, or publishing X articles in Y years, we define exactly what we need to do. Yes, we already know what we need to do, but these goal-setting conversations reveal our understanding of how we're going to get there. They can also expose misconceptions and over-reaching – the habit of trying to do too much – and develop ways of resolving these potential barriers to regular, paced writing. We can see some of this going on in a form of self-negotiation in the example above, but it is important to remember that this planning and monitoring would also be the subject of brief discussions at the start and end of the day, along with informal discussions during breaks.

Finally – to emphasise – there is literally no point in setting goals without monitoring the extent to which they were achieved. In performative settings, where work is measured in so many ways already, this may sound like just another form of surveillance. In fact, it is the opposite: monitoring our outputs lets us learn about what we are actually doing in the writing process.

Peer-formativity

There are many researchers, academics and professionals who want to write, and there are many of those who write want to write more. Choosing not to engage with systems for regulating academic writing may stop us producing in ways that are valued by institutions, and, as a result, we may not produce in ways that we value. A resulting 'feeling of constant low grade failure', as one participant in the writing meeting study put it, may compound this effect, as the connection between writing that counts in these systems and writing that counts in personal terms is broken.

There are those who see the whole performative apparatus generally and research assessment specifically as nothing – literally nothing – more than a device to preserve privilege and power in a few institutions and/or for a few individuals. The implication that the individual will never acquire sufficient power in/ through writing must be challenged; having writing meetings is one way for those who want to write, working together as writing peers, to make that challenge.

This is not, therefore, about providing an extra layer of monitoring to feed into performative systems; the writing meeting is a framework for individuals to set writing goals that align with their own values and to take time to consider – in conversations with others – how or if they can align these values with institutional values and meet collective goals.

The components of social writing deployed in writing meetings are:

- discussing the personal and collective benefits of writing and drawbacks of not writing;
- developing peer-formative relationships and interactions; and
- mutually supporting the intention to change writing behaviours.

This is not to say that all the tensions and ambivalences identified at the start of this chapter will go away. Tensions may still flare up. All the more reason to have supporting structures and relationships in place. While the writing meeting can bridge the gap between external goals and personal values, it cannot prevent this gap from opening up again. In fact, anticipating when such a gap might open up again and what you might do to stop it interfering with your writing would be a useful talking point for the kind of writing meeting described in this chapter. This would not, of course, mean simply talking about the gap, but also setting goals for bridging it. The strength of the writing meeting structure and template is that it will keep this discussion focused on issues and strategies for dealing with them. It will also prompt review of the extent to which the strategy succeeded.

The writing meeting is a way of engaging with performativity in this sense and to this extent. Since it is not formally a part of the system, it may be seen as another form of disengagement from the system, even when we meet institution-ally approved writing targets.

This is not, therefore, a manifesto for disengaging from the system, but it may mean disengaging from other roles and tasks in order to engage in writing, which is the subject of the next chapter.

Chapter 7

Disengagement

The concept of disengagement has been linked to productive writing. Mayrath (2008) argued that disengagement is a function of writing, in the sense that it is a factor in the highly productive writing practices required for regular publication in high quality academic journals. He surveyed some of the top researchers in his field:

> All of the surveyed authors are extremely busy with institutional duties, meetings with graduate students, teaching classes, responding to emails from colleagues and students around the country, and, of course, maintaining a personal life at home. Thus, to produce academic work they must isolate themselves and block out distractions.
>
> (Mayrath 2008: 51)

My research suggests that disengagement is, indeed, perceived as a component of productive writing, as this extract from one of the questionnaire responses in my study (Murray 2013a) shows:

> Disengaging is quite an important part of my repertoire of writing habits. To me it means 'disconnecting' with other responsibilities in order to achieve a deeper level of focus on my writing, which requires me to bring all my attention and energy to bear on the tasks that it involves (thinking, formulating, experimenting, drafting, reflecting, reading, synthesising, generating ideas, pulling together a lot of information, drawing out key themes, articulating complex ideas, adopting positions, generating explanations, reaching conclusions etc.). I guess the point is that academic writing requires so many different competencies and skills that you need, metaphorically, to clear your desk. This means switching off both physically and psychologically in order to be able to write properly.
>
> (Anonymous interviewee in Murray 2013a: 85)

However, while disengagement is a potential mechanism in academic writing, it is not essential for those who want to write to 'isolate' themselves. This is not the only way. Disengaging need not be a solitary process, since peer interactions are often a component of disengagement. In fact, in some instances, peer support will sustain disengagement from other tasks in order to write, as previous chapters have shown.

Disengagement can have a number of meanings and motivations. It can signal ambivalence about other tasks, or about writing itself. It may involve ignoring or severing connections with other roles. There can be ambivalence towards the imperative to produce writing that has to be accounted for – and in many cases steered towards – assessment systems that value some forms of research and writing more than others. For the purposes of this chapter, disengagement is less about these forms of ambivalence than about how it is possible to privilege writing over other tasks. Disengagement has not been fully explored in these terms or in this context. Nor has it been theorised in this way, in relation to academic writing.

Key messages:

- It is necessary to disengage from other tasks in order to focus on writing.
- *Disengagement from* other tasks in order to write may be more constructively reconceptualised as *engagement with* writing.
- Relationships around writing enable three moves: (1) from guilt and anxiety to legitimising writing, (2) from competition to social writing and (3) from not writing at work to dedicating time at work to write.

This chapter explores both the value and risk of disengaging from other activities in order to write. For many, disengagement – crucial as they believe it to be for their writing – is a luxury rather than a routine. Some find it impossible to disengage from other duties or – and this is very common – from the internet, email and social media. Where the time required to produce academic writing is undefined – and it seems that it usually is – there is increased pressure on the individual to solve the problem, and a risk that those who critique this state or struggle to perform in this context may be 'cast . . . as people who are failing to cope' (Barcan 2013: 8).

This chapter defines the concept of disengagement and explains its relevance to academic writing. It describes different levels of disengagement that academics and professionals say make it possible to do academic writing. It deploys scarcity theory to examine the problem further: when time is limited, scarcity theory suggests, there is reduced 'bandwidth' not only for the act of writing, but also for working out how to solve the problem of finding time for writing in workloads, particularly those that do not allocate time for writing. Scarcity theory allows us to explore both the individual and institutional components of this problem. This chapter concludes with a model for moving from disengagement to engagement:

disengagement *from* other tasks in order to write is reconceptualised as engagement *with* writing.

Privileging writing – 'It is not a hobby'

> I do find the retreats and Writing for Publication programme really useful . . . despite my unsuccessful attempts at disengagement the last few times. It's work, it's seen as valid – I don't feel like I am skiving off! . . . Structured interventions afford participants the opportunity to be somewhere for something they have signed up for. It pushes writing up the agenda. But I also think that the institution must offer structured support to writing within the working day. It is not a hobby. Publications are hugely important for the academic, the department and the institution. The onus should not be on the academic to publish without providing them time to do so. A colleague in another University and her fellow lecturers in the centre have one writing day per week allowed for their writing. Now this would be ideal!

This response from a participant in my study (Murray 2013a: 84, 90) suggests that for writing to occur, the individual must be committed to writing and must put writing 'on the agenda' and thereby establish its importance, but institutions do not provide a mechanism for this. How does an individual develop capacity to operate in this setting? Will this not limit the individual's capacity to disengage from other tasks in order to engage with writing? What about those who are ambivalent about disengaging from these other tasks?

How do productive writers manage it? Mayrath (2008) showed that highly productive academics in educational psychology moved between teaching, research and administration in a series of engagements and disengagements:

> I think the key to academic productivity is the ability to ignore, screen out, and avoid distractions. Scientific work takes great concentration – sustained concentration. The enemy of research is the modern world of emails, cell calls, faxes, endless committee meetings . . . and all the wheels and gears of modern bureaucracies.
>
> (Mayrath 2008: 52)

Hartley and Branthwaite (1989) offer many useful practical tips and, since they have a background in psychology, and since their research looked at writing practices used by psychologists, they integrate practical and behavioural strategies. However, most of their suggestions are for the individual writer. Apart from getting feedback on drafts, there is nothing about developing writing-oriented conversations and relationships.

The potential impact of the absence of writing-oriented interactions and relationships in inhibiting writing was established in earlier chapters. This can lead to disengagement from writing, to the separation of writing from other research and professional tasks. In this way, writing comes to be seen as distinct from other activities, requiring different types of time and even covert practice: 'I prefer to write in spaces and times when nobody knows what I'm up to . . . I diarise writing as meeting-free days rather than writing days'. This may be one of the reasons why writing remains secret, knowledge about writing remains tacit and real time for writing remains unstable.

Choosing to disengage

My study set out to explore whether people could relate to this concept of disengagement that seemed so crucial for productive academic writing: *is* academic writing associated with disengagement (Murray 2013a)? If it turned out that it was, I wanted to know more about how people did their disengagement: how did they interpret and perform it? For anyone who did relate to the concept of disengagement in this context, I also wanted to ask how effective they thought they were at disengaging.

An email questionnaire elicited responses from academics, researchers and professionals across the UK in a range of disciplines, at a range of universities and a few other organisations – a wider range of responses than in Mayrath's study. Quotations in this chapter are from participants in this study, unless otherwise stated.

Everyone in my study associated disengagement with academic writing. Clearly, this response could have been influenced by the fact that they had been asked questions about disengagement – but the strength of respondents' statements and the level of detail in their descriptions of their writing practices suggest otherwise. Of course, it could also be that those who chose to respond were predisposed towards disengagement, while those who did not recognise or practise it did not respond. However, the range of disciplines and the unanimity of their responses made this finding worth thinking about.

Disengaging from other roles, tasks, responsibilities in order to write was defined by participants in three ways: physical, cognitive and social disengagement. Clearly, there can be overlap between these, as each may be implicated in the others, but it is helpful to shed some light on what is happening to begin by considering them separately.

- *Physical disengagement* was defined as clearing time in the diary, clearing the desk of unfinished work and finding a place to write. This was seen as the simplest form of disengagement. It was easy if it involved writing at home, but this was difficult for those with children and/or caring responsibilities. It was impossible for those who could not write off-campus:

  'It is important to have a physical space which is conducive to writing – I would never try to do it in my office on campus. So this is usually in my study at home. I surround myself with the relevant books and journal publications needed for my writing task and make sure that, as far as possible, I will be uninterrupted. I ensure that I have attended to all other immediate deadlines and VERY pressing tasks before sitting down to write.'

They all agreed that writing needs uninterrupted time, but that this type of time is never available in their workplaces. Many only have uninterrupted time for writing at home. Many use their annual leave to write. This suggests that writing does indeed need to be performed away from other tasks, since any other task may displace writing, or that it is perceived in this way.

In all the workplaces represented in this study, other activities have the potential to be prioritised over writing. Physically disengaging from other tasks and other places is a concrete way to engage in writing. This was seen as essential, but other forms of disengagement are needed to make it work.

- *Cognitive disengagement* was defined as psychologically preparing to concentrate on writing. This was seen as the most complex and difficult form of disengagement. Some felt that they had, as one put it, 'a strong capacity to switch off from other demands of the job', but others found that they continually had to legitimise their writing.

  'Creativity and writing often need time to emerge, unconfused by stresses and demands of day-to-day work. For me, disengaging would be to take a block of time, or shorter blocks of time during which I was psychologically free to get on with the task of writing something.'

Some said they were not good at this and attributed their failures to organisational working practices, such as the imperative to attend meetings and the distribution of teaching throughout the year, in evenings and at weekends and the absence of writing in workload models.

- *Social disengagement* was defined as separating oneself from other people's demands in order to write, while accepting that this might meet with disapproval, and engaging with other writers so as to sustain this approach:

  'It helps to "care less". If someone is desperate to speak to me or have me do something, they can usually wait, but it took me some years to realise I was not indispensable – or at least that jobs could equally well be done later.

  One has to protect oneself and be totally "selfish". In post-92 universities there is really not a lot of space and support for research and academic writing. If one does not want to kill oneself with 80-hour weeks, one has to cut corners somewhere. This means doing an average (or even a poor) job with teaching to free up time for research and academic writing. One also has to get over the fact that others will be jealous, if one is successful or if one has a research allowance. Therefore, my aim is to enjoy my work as much as I can. I do the research I like and I do the writing I want to do. This attitude helps when it comes to setting time aside for research and writing and sticking to it at the cost of being unhelpful to others.'

In addition to providing these accounts of disengagement, they listed, unprompted, various forms of social writing that they used to sustain their writing:

- writing group sessions
- peer group review
- peer support
- writing retreats
- a writer's sanctuary
- a course or workshop
- mentor
- buddy
- writing with colleagues and co-authors
- networking with other writers, forming a community of writers
- collaborative research.

This list illustrates many different types of engagement with others who write, defined by these participants as an essential component of productive academic writing.

In this sense, for these respondents, ignoring other people's demands in order to write is accompanied by the development of relationships with others who write. This might seem like a suspension of collegiality in one area of their work in order to work collegially in another. This can be interpreted as an individual choice, which it is, but there are institutional factors to be taken into account in interpreting these writers' experiences.

The problem is that while the components of many workplace roles and tasks are well defined, the place of writing is not. The problem, therefore, should not simply be attributed to individual selfishness but to disengagement with the act of writing as institutionally constructed: as long as institutions do not make the *act of writing* visible and valuable, it is likely to be contested. Moreover, it is likely to become the scene of contests between tasks, role and individuals. Making written *outputs* valuable and visible does not really address this problem; it may, in fact, exacerbate it by increasing the pressure to produce without articulating the process of production.

Scarcity theory: is lack of time *really* the problem?

> Scarcity captures the mind . . . when we experience scarcity of any kind, we become absorbed by it. The mind orients automatically, powerfully, toward unfulfilled needs. . . . It changes how we think.
>
> (Mullainathan and Shafir 2013: 7)

What seems to be the prevailing condition of scarcity of time for writing prompted me to consider using scarcity theory to analyse the problem. We all understand, I assume, that 'lack of time' – for writing or for any other task – is a complex construction, with many individual and organisational components. We know that it's about prioritising, and we understand that it's not as simple as just adjusting priorities. It is not always possible to prioritise the act of writing. Scarcity theory provides another angle from which to explore this problem. In fact, it may explain how scarcity of time for writing became a problem in the first place.

The theory says that scarcity can alter 'how we interpret the world' and 'shape our choices and our . . . behaviours'. It 'leads to dissatisfaction and struggle' (Mullainathan and Shafir 2013: 9 and 12). Scarcity means not looking ahead, not weighing options, perhaps not even seeing options. More importantly, scarcity theory argues that this mechanism works on all other mechanisms, including personality and environment.

Scarcity can therefore be a mindset: 'it changes how we think' and 'affects what we notice, how we weigh our choices, how we deliberate, and ultimately what we decide and how we behave' (Mullainathan and Shafir 2013: 12). If, as the authors argue, scarcity – and its effects – are beyond our personal control, is this another argument for recruiting social processes?

If we apply scarcity theory to writing, should we think in terms of scarcity of time for writing as focusing our attention on the need for more time, rather than on how we might change our writing habits? Could scarcity theory explain why writing is such a problem? Does scarcity of time impinge on our ability to write – does having limited time for writing limit our development as writers and limit our development through writing? Is scarcity working subconsciously, forcing us to focus on the problem rather than looking at how we might solve it? Is this an argument for stepping back and thinking about different ways of writing – can social writing provide not just a backdrop but a mechanism for changing writing concepts and behaviours? If scarcity changes someone's mindset about academic writing, can social writing change it back?

In order to see if the components of scarcity theory would be helpful in analysing the problem of writing and suggesting directions for engaging with writing, the following sections draw on Mullainathan and Shafir's (2013) account. This allows us to explore academic writing from a different angle and to develop another theoretical rationale for social writing.

- Scarcity reduces the 'mental bandwidth' available for thinking about a problem: 'Because we are preoccupied by scarcity, because our minds constantly return to it, we have less mind to give to the rest of life' (Mullainathan and Shafir 2013: 13). This results in reduced insight, less forward thinking and limited active management of activity, which, in turn, leads to further scarcity.

  o This might explain the experience of 'non-writers' – their scarcity of time for writing perpetuated that scarcity. This concept could explain why people are immediately so productive in social writing settings: mental bandwidth available for writing is immediately increased. The use of structure and communal writing, moreover, increases self-control, which is often undermined by scarcity.

- Scarcity of time leads to 'persistent time concerns' (p. 63).

  o This might explain the constant focus on time and associated interpersonal concerns, in settings where social processes are not overt or visible for writing, although they are overt and visible for other tasks and roles. Lack of time and failure to make time for writing could be seen as the 'predictable consequences of overtaxed bandwidth' (p. 162).

- Scarcity leads to diminished self-control and increases impulsive behaviours.

  o This may explain why there is so much discussion of the positive impact of 'discipline' and 'structure' at writing retreats, for example. It may also explain the inability to quit email – and other tasks that prevent writing.

- The problem is not with the individual, although it might look that way. It might appear to be 'lack of skill, no motivation, or insufficient education' (p. 65).

  o This might explain why academics and professionals are unable to write as often as they want to. Moreover, in settings where writing time and relationships are not overt, the act of writing may itself evoke scarcity.

- The concept of 'granularity' may explain why writing in the fixed programme of sessions, in short increments of time (e.g. sixty or ninety minutes), may be so helpful. Writing in long stretches of time is more complex; writing in short sessions makes managing the complexity of writing easier. Writers can thereby *make* writing more 'granular'.

- Scarcity leads to poverty; it's not the other way round.

  o This might explain why lack of time for writing heightens focus on other activities, such as teaching or patient care – which are, of course, important – and reduces focus on writing, so that it becomes invisible, impossible. In this sense, it could be argued that we are active players in the invisibility of writing in academic and professional settings. However, if we continue to apply the theory, scarcity, by changing our thinking and behaviour, will make us unaware of this. In this way, it is argued, scarcity creates myopia. This suggests that we will have limited perspective on writing. Social writing settings, by contrast, involve putting writing and writers in new contexts, where they interact with other views and where there is potential for an expanding rather than limited vision. This may be why writing looks and feels so different so quickly in social writing workshops, groups and retreats. People quickly see that there *is* time to write.

- The solution is to build in 'slack' and 'buffering against shocks' (p. 137), which sounds a little like the step in the writing meeting for anticipating barriers to writing in the previous chapter.

If we apply scarcity theory to accounts of writing, we can see the difficulty of finding sufficient focus to write as a problem of lack of 'bandwidth':

> To me, [disengaging] means getting into the zone, actually sitting down and committing a high percentage of your thoughts to the task at hand. Too often, when one is reading, you are thinking about the text, or even other things. When you are writing you use a different thought process, not the understanding side of things, but rather the creative. This thought process needs to be turned on, and in order to do this you need to disengage from other tasks, so that they do not distract you, as this process is very thought intensive.

This definition of the need for 'committing a high percentage of your thoughts' suggests that academic writing can be accounted for in this way.

This account also makes it clear how scarcity stops us thinking about our values and our actions in a strategic way – or does it show that even those who are still able to think about writing in a strategic way may not be able to act on that thinking? This analysis points up a potential link to passive acceptance of the conditions of competitive writing, paralysis of the ability to create time and space for writing and inertia in groups. Where neither time nor social processes for writing are overt, this creates the condition of scarcity. More importantly, this suggests that those who experience scarcity of time for writing are more likely to be less effective at writing, not because they are less capable in writing but because scarcity reduces their ability to recruit their capacity.

On the positive side, scarcity creates focus, in the way that deadlines, for example, will produce writing: 'Scarcity allows us to do something we could not easily do on our own' (p. 26). Over time, however, this focus can lead to overlooking other options and to tunnel vision, which may, in turn, inhibit writing capacity or the ability to access capacity.

Our behaviours are not, therefore, always, neatly aligned with our preferences or our goals, which is why deliberately trying to align our actions with our goals was the focus of the previous chapter. This concept is challenging for those who are clear thinkers and motivated professionals; can we really be so confused about our goals and actions? Can we really be so blocked in trying to achieve them? Our goals are so obvious and often so fixed and public that it seems absurd to be defining any kind of a gap between personal and organisational goals and processes for achieving them. Surely, it is simply up to us to bridge this gap? However, perhaps the gap is not between our goals and actions but between our goals and our capacity to focus on them in the condition of scarcity?

In addition to scarcity of time for writing, perhaps we can think of scarcity in terms of relationships around writing, in the sense of a scarcity of allies and colleagues in the practice of writing. In some workplaces there can even be hostility towards those who write – as shown in references to an earlier study in an earlier chapter – and the general competitiveness of writing for publication is part of the culture that can inhibit collegiality and collaboration in writing. In fact, this can inhibit collegiality in other roles (Barcan 2013). Does scarcity theory, in this sense, explain all the references in so many interviews to the experience that 'we are all in the same boat'? Initially, this seems like just another comment on the supportive atmosphere of writer's groups and writing retreats, but perhaps it expresses recognition of a mutually reinforcing process. Perhaps it conveys the importance of writing in these ways for addressing scarcity of writing-oriented relationships?

Having used scarcity theory in this way to analyse the problem of the insufficiency of writing time, can we develop a 'sufficiency' theory? Instead of 'why having too little means so much' – the subtitle of Mullainathan and Shafir's (2013) book on scarcity theory – should we be thinking about 'Why having *enough* time means so much?' Does scarcity theory help us to understand why environments that create and structure time for writing make such a difference? What would be the components or conditions of sufficiency theory? – to increase 'bandwidth' for thinking about writing, not so much developing writing capacity as increasing the capacity that is made available for writing, and only for writing. This could increase self-control and reduce impulsive responses, in the way that we know happens in groups and retreats. This may explain why social writing may work where individual effort fails. It may explain why writing workshops using social writing principles are experienced as transformative: they not only provide an opportunity to step back and review concepts and practices but also introduce new practices and initiate new conversations and relationships around writing.

So, *is* lack of time the problem? Yes, it is, in the sense that scarcity of time produces problematic effects that were not previously defined in this way. The problem is, however, much more complex than poor time management. Scarcity theory offers a different explanation of the problem: time scarcity changes how we think and act, and that is what causes the problem.

A model for engaging with writing

The focus of this chapter – the idea of disengaging from other tasks in order to engage with writing – may seem like a negative construction, but there is a positive construction: those who disengaged found ways to construct the focus they needed to write and were actively engaging with others who were writing Moreover, they saw that engagement with others as part of their engagement with writing.

Drawing on participants' responses, I developed a model to show the components of disengagement and the move – made by many of these respondents – from disengaging from other tasks to engaging with writing:

- through physical engagement – moving from writing at work – or not – to dedicated writing time and space;
- through cognitive engagement – moving from fear and anxiety to legitimising writing;
- through social engagement – moving from competition to social writing activities.

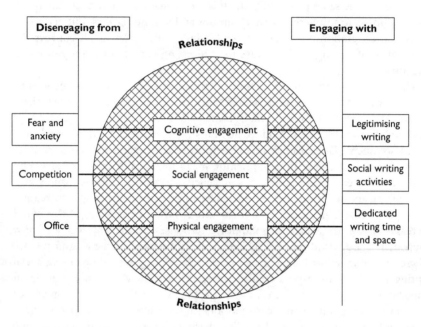

Figure 7.1 A model for engaging with writing

This model may help us understand why some people, if they are positioned on the left-hand-side of the diagram in Figure 7.1, become overwhelmed by writing-related anxiety, lack of confidence and/or competing tasks and peers.

This model suggests that those who do not write might not, in fact, lack writing skills or research capacity; it may be that what is lacking is the social structure within which to construct this move to engaging with writing.

It could be argued that trying to write in environments that are designed for other, very different activities is bound to fail, not because of individual deficiency or inability to cope, but because writing requires physical, cognitive and/or social engagement.

Conclusion

> Clearing my head of other priorities and issues crowding in. It's mainly in the head.
>
> (Questionnaire response)

Is the ability to focus on writing 'mainly in the head'? Is it entirely internal – is it an 'ability'? Do we develop that – or not – in the course of our work, or should we work specifically on that ability to maintain it? Is this oversimplifying a complex social process? Of course, our ability to write does come back to an individual's conscious goals and intentions, but are these not shaped by institutional norms, resources and relationships?

It seemed, from earlier stages in my argument, in previous chapters, that there were, indeed, strategies we could use to create and protect time to write. In fact, many of the social writing activities described in this book were initially developed to address the problem of lack of time for writing. There is evidence that they did help, and even that strategies for changing writing time were useful for other research and professional tasks.

However, these chapters showed that social writing did much more than help people to create writing time. They began to develop understanding of the social components of writing, and explained why not attending to these social components could be problematic.

Scarcity theory provided another way of explaining this. It raised the question of what the experience of time scarcity might be doing to shape our thoughts and actions. Scarcity theory helpfully defines the problem not in terms of individual or institutional deficiencies but in terms of a mindset that social processes can work on. My argument is that time and space are not the issue – other people can help us access the high bandwidth we need for writing.

Disengagement – in the sense of removing ourselves from certain places or meetings – is not the whole answer. We still have to come back to those places and meetings. However, the act of engagement – and the associated engagement – does involve individual agency, and this keeps people writing.

But how do we integrate this agency in the workplace? We need to extend the concept of 'workplace' beyond the physical location of our work. The workplace of writing is much wider, and writing relationships are not always established in that location. They can be anywhere. As long as institutions do not account for time and space dedicated to these relationships, perhaps they will continue to seem and feel separate from what will still be thought of as the workplace. As one participant in my disengagement study put it, there should be 'more institutional support for the fact, act and art of writing'. Otherwise, only those who disengage will write, and some are unable and/or unwilling to do that.

Have institutions disengaged from writing? Is that the problem? Is there a covert elitism that sustains and is sustained by the culture in which writing is invisible and unspeakable?

The components of social writing involved in disengagement are:

- cognitive, social and/or physical disengagement from other tasks in order to write in the company of others who want to write;
- disengaging from those who see focusing on writing as selfish;
- developing the concept of sufficiency of time for writing; and
- working with others to protect the 'high bandwidth' required for academic writing.

The starting point for this chapter was the finding that individuals – including those who are the most productive and successful in their field – see their writing as a series of disengagements and engagements.

A key point of this chapter is that disengagement does occur and that we need to explore what that means and why it happens and how to deal with it.

The conclusion is that we have not fully explored the complexity of this process; it might not be straightforward for everyone, and even when we do disengage from other activities in order to write, sometimes that only increases anxiety.

This chapter has not fully explored the anxiety that may be associated with disengagement. The next chapter explains how social writing can provide a supporting structure for these engagements, a structure that can contain writing-related anxiety.

Chapter 8

Containment

Social writing as containment

> Inherent in every task – and institutions are set up to perform specific tasks –
> there is the anxiety, pain and confusion arising from attempting to perform
> the task; and . . . institutions defend themselves against this anxiety by struc-
> turing themselves, their working practices and ultimately their staff relation-
> ships so as to unconsciously defend themselves against the anxiety inherent
> in the task.
>
> (Obholzer 1986: 202)

For anyone coming across the concept of containment for the first time, it might
seem strange or out of place in a discussion of writing. Surely writing is about
exploration rather than containment? Could containment not be misconstrued as
control or interpreted as the imposition of restraint on our writing? Will this trigger resistance or anxiety, both understandable when faced with a new concept,
particularly since writing itself evokes anxiety for many?

Not everyone experiences 'anxiety, pain and confusion' around writing; writing will not inevitably provoke these responses for everyone. In fact, it is impossible to capture everyone's emotions towards writing in one definition. However,
it is safe to assume that most of us have felt anxious about our writing at some
time. This may be anxiety about whether we can perform a writing task to the
required standard, or it may be about whether we will find time to write. There
may be many different triggers for anxiety, and these may vary from time to time
for each individual, depending on the nature of the writing task and/or on other
demands on their time.

However, perhaps we need to look more closely at the interface between our
writing and the institutions where we work. If we apply Obholzer's principles,
writing is the 'task' that these institutions 'structure', primarily in terms of written
outputs. Does this mean that institutions are structuring themselves in such a way
as to 'defend themselves' from writing-related anxiety? Do they transfer anxiety
to those who want to write or should be writing? Are staff relationships structured
so as to defend the institution from anxiety?

This analysis risks putting the institution and its staff at odds, but that is how writing is experienced by many people: they do not see and cannot find a place to write in their workplaces. We saw in earlier chapters how rare it is for academics and professionals who write to feel supported by their institutions. This perspective is, therefore, worth thinking about further. If this is a problem, we should be looking for ways to address it rather than avoid it:

> I was aware at the writer's retreat of the frustration, of feeling that you were attempting to achieve something that was very challenging, and I support the intensity of the writer's retreat which meant that on a consistent basis you were having to face that frustration over the course of the weekend, whereas in daily practice, instead of facing that frustration, I think I avoid it sometimes.

Key messages:

- Levels of anxiety around writing can be debilitating.
- Writing is one of many competing tasks in our workloads. Managing competing tasks in order to write and publish to the highest standards can be stressful for novice and experienced writers.
- Healthy organisational cultures will have structures and processes that support the management of anxiety associated with writing.
- We can develop structures and processes to contain writing-related anxiety and make writing the primary task.
- Raising unconscious processes to a conscious level provides clarity in thinking about writing, and this facilitates writing.

This chapter explores the concept of containment, using the components of holistic containment to define healthy organisational cultures and illustrating containment by drawing on writers' comments in one of my studies (MacLeod *et al.* 2012; Murray *et al.* 2012). The aim is to explain how social writing works as containment and to use containment theory to explain how social writing works.

Containment theory

The focus of this chapter originated at one of my structured writing retreats, when participants suggested that the retreats were a form of containment. Containment is about the processes that enable people to manage (contain) unmanageable (uncontainable) thoughts, feelings and experiences. Containment theory has been applied in many settings, such as social work (Toasland 2007), social work education (Ruch 2005, 2007; Ward 2008) and business (Kahn 2001). We used this theory to re-analyse data in one of my studies to see if it would explain how structured writing retreats work (MacLeod *et al.* 2012; Murray *et al.* 2012). Our analysis showed that these retreats worked by:

- making writing the primary task
- preventing anti-task behaviour
- containing writing-related anxiety.

Containment theory helps to explain why it is that we can be productive in social writing and why we might be less productive, and more anxious about our writing, in other uncontained settings. Where there is anxiety about writing, this will impinge on concentration and other processes. Where writing is not the primary task, it will be more difficult to find time and space to do it. Where there is anti-task behaviour – which people often describe in terms of procrastination or displacement activities – we may not actually get down to writing at all. Containment theory therefore explains some of the conditions needed for writing and some of the factors that inhibit it.

This theory also allows us to consider organisational processes. Many institutions will not have put in place structures and processes that support writing. There may be sources of support for student writing, but not for staff. In fact, there may be no reference to the act of writing at all in institutional workloads, procedures and discourses:

> talking about faculty work without referring to writing says something about what the university is sponsoring. . . . Eliminating the word 'writing' from a discussion of faculty work also implies that the process one engages in to produce a published research manuscript is less meaningful than the fact of publication itself, eliding the hard work faculty do to achieve publication.
>
> (Salem and Follett 2013: 57)

Lack of discussion of this important component of academic and professional work may create or intensify anxiety and frustration. Even defining this as a 'problem' may be problematic. If we are just meant to get on with the writing, what is the purpose of talking about it? If it is a crucial part of our work, what is there to talk about? Do we really want to be 'contained' in our writing?

However, if uncontained emotions, like anxiety, are likely to disrupt writing, we need to think about and put in place ways of containing emotions. This does not mean that we should deny or neutralise them and turn into writing robots; instead, it means finding a way of working that will prevent anxiety and frustration impinging on our writing. Without some way of containing anxiety – the theory tells us – clear thinking is not possible, and we will not write.

Holistic containment

The concept of holistic containment provides a useful framework for exploring all the facets of containment:

- *emotional containment* looks at how unmanageable feelings may be made manageable;
- *organisational containment* focuses on organisational policies, procedures and day-to-day practices that contribute to organisational, professional and managerial clarity; and
- *epistemological containment* looks at settings where individuals can make sense of complexity, manage uncertainty and achieve clarity in their work.

Holistic containment, therefore, combines the institutional and the individual. In order to define these facets further, we developed the following codes for analysing interview transcripts:

- 'Primary task' refers a task or duty you associate with your work role, where that task has primacy over other tasks within your role.
- 'Anti-task' refers to an activity, conscious or unconscious, that stops you doing the primary task and defends you against anxiety you associate with that task.
- 'Anxiety' refers to fear, unease or uncertainty that you associate with performance of that task.
- 'Emotional containment' refers to experience of retreats that help you think about or manage unmanageable feelings.
- 'Organisational containment' refers to retreat practices that increase organisational, professional and managerial clarity.
- 'Epistemological containment' refers to experiences of retreats that help you to make sense of your writing projects, your approach to writing and seeing your writing as central to your role.
- 'Holistic containment' (Ruch 2005) refers to experiences of retreats that integrate the three dimensions of containment: emotional, organisational and epistemological (adapted from MacLeod *et al.* 2012: 646).

This is not how we normally talk about writing. Holistic containment may strike some as an odd construct or unwieldy jargon for talking about something we understand pretty well already. However, I contend that we may know a lot about writing but it will be more or less absent from our discussions of our work.

Even when we talk about 'writing' it is unlikely that we will talk about the act of writing. For that reason, talking about writing is very much a feature of this chapter: on a very simple level, containment theory gives us another way of talking about writing, and it explains why writing may be more complex than we think it should be, given how much we already know about it.

Making writing the primary task

Writing is almost never defined as the primary task. It usually competes with many other tasks, in a competition that it usually loses. This is perhaps why it is so difficult to make time to write: even when we make time to write, we are acutely aware of other tasks we are not doing. It is easy to see how this can limit our capacity for clarity in thinking, writing and thinking about writing.

In containment theory, an organisation's primary task is defined as the task that it must do in order to survive (Menzies-Lyth 1988). Where the primary task is clear to everyone in the organisation, members of that organisation are likely to focus on that task and find meaning and satisfaction in performing it. Where the primary task is not clear, there is likely to be confusion and conflict. This confusion makes it more likely that individuals in the organisation will experience anxiety and use social defences against the task. They will find ways to avoid it, but may not realise they are doing so.

In universities and professional workplaces, there is not one primary task but many competing tasks (Barnett 1999). Several of these may be given primacy at different times, or at any time. The pattern of primacy, so to speak, may be predictable or unpredictable. An organisation should manage this process, but in practice it seems to be up to the individual to 'work harder and longer' (Acker and Armenti 2004: 16) or find their individual route around or personal strategy for negotiating this complexity (Clegg 2008). Since writing is not identified in these terms by the institution, the onus falls on the individual. However, putting the onus on the individual to manage complexity is likely to increase anxiety. The demands of all the tasks are legitimate, but the individual cannot perform them all at once.

Making writing the primary task does not mean neglecting other tasks, though it can feel like that in settings where there is no organisational position for writing. It seems that we have to be able to make writing the primary task some of the time; other tasks will have primacy at other times.

Preventing anti-task behaviour

Anti-task behaviour comes with confusion about and conflict between tasks. It refers to any unconscious behaviour that is used as a defence against anxiety related to the task, and it inhibits performance of the primary task. In order to consciously focus on the primary task, we would need to know what it was, and there would need to be general agreement in the organisation about our primary task. Because it is not clear what the primary task is, at any given time, anxiety persists. It will even, for some, become chronic.

If it seems absurd to be proposing that the primary task of a university, service or hospital is unclear, there is still the question of where writing fits – is writing the primary task in these organisations? When and where is it the primary task? Even if these terms are not used, how is the role of writing in our professional work defined? Even in workplaces where publications are highly valued, writing is not the primary task of these organisations. In this context, anti-task behaviour is likely.

Using containment theory in this way explains why it is so difficult for the individual to focus on writing. It explains why individuals find it so difficult – often impossible – to privilege writing over other professional roles and tasks.

Containing writing-related anxiety

It is well established that academics and professionals experience anxiety in relation to writing (Moore 2003). We know that negative cognitions may be associated with writing (Boice 1987a). Sometimes this is referred to as 'writer's block', but it may also be seen in failure to achieve personal goals. Shame and perfectionism may be associated with writing (Grant and Knowles 2000). There can be tensions between different forms of publication, and aspirations to write in different forms, to have different types of 'impact', even for experienced and eminent writers (Carnell *et al.* 2008). The greatest anxiety, however, presents as a lack of time for writing, leading to feelings of guilt, fear and dread being associated with writing projects. While these are individual emotions, the organisation plays a role in triggering them. The interaction of the organisational and the personal – or extrinsic and intrinsic motivation – complicates it further.

The position of writing in organisations may therefore be a problem – it is not just a matter of individual laziness, weakness or lack of confidence. It is not just about poor time management. If the organisation does not identify writing as the primary task, there will be writing-related anxiety. The positioning of writing in organisations is the problem, particularly if there are no mechanisms for discussing it:

> Where there are no mechanisms within the organisation for a reflexive exploration of task complexity, theory predicts that the anxiety that task confusion elicits will be evidenced in the construction of social defences that are observable in the day-to-day practices of staff.
>
> (MacLeod *et al.* 2012: 644)

How do we construct 'social defences' in our day-to-day practices? Could not finding time to write be one of them? Will social writing – as described in this chapter and throughout this book – be any different? In a sense, social writing is about making writing the primary task, but it may not address the organisational problem. To what extent can social writing create organisational clarity about primary task? People regularly say that when their institution pays for them to attend retreats they feel valued, for example, so perhaps this is a way of providing clarity about the primary task. If the organisation pays, it can be seen as an acknowledgement that writing is the primary task for that period.

Understanding of the problem of writing in this way is an important part of making writing the primary task. The writing retreat provides a structure and process that organisations can put in place to help people manage writing-related anxiety and negotiate task complexity. This is a containment process.

The specific terms that people use to define writing-related anxiety suggest the need for containment. For example, not wanting to stop writing at the end of a writing session, for fear of not being able to start again, might be seen as lack of confidence, but using containment theory we can see this as linked to the lack of organisational containment of writing. There is also the period of anxiety just before starting to write, which might be seen as fear of high-stakes peer review, but could also be linked to the difficulty of making writing the primary task. Given the fluidity of the position of writing in many workplaces, it may be that the perfectionism that many professionals and academics report is not so much the cause of anxiety as the result of the anxiety generated by writing being uncontained.

We all know that our writing will go through numerous drafts and require revisions after peer review, but if all those stages are not defined as the primary task, when do we do them? This might explain the frustration that people express in relation to their writing – frustration that seems to be triggered by the act of writing (and re-writing) but perhaps relates to writing being uncontained. It is easy to see this as an individual problem, rather than a problem with writing itself. Compounding this may be the fear of being misunderstood in this way, thus further inhibiting discussion of writing and its place in our work.

Structured writing retreats contain anxiety by creating a structure for writing sessions, and this, in turn, limits writing-related anxiety, while goal setting and monitoring reinforce the sense of incremental achievement with writing. Goal setting and monitoring also increase self-efficacy in relation to writing, as described in a previous chapter. The social support of others contains anxieties during the act of writing. Social support in this context refers to the impact of writing with others who are prepared to change their writing habits and are willing to discuss their writing practices. This contains anxieties about not only the planning and monitoring of writing but also about the quality of the writing and the writer's ability to solve problems in their writing.

Constructing containment

A containing environment, therefore, can help us negotiate competing tasks and find ways to make writing the primary task. But writing is still an individual act. How do individuals construct containment?

The experience of a structured writing retreat helps people see that they can write. Almost immediately, the anxiety is reduced or removed entirely. They start to achieve their writing goals from the start. They achieve much more than they thought they would. They see that when writing is the primary task, they get on with it. Because they set and monitor their own writing goals, there is likely to be individual agency for everyone in their writing. Because they develop confidence in this process, they are likely to develop competence in making writing the primary task in other environments, after a retreat.

The structure of the retreat day, with its fixed timeslots – provides a form of containment. It makes writing the focus of the day, and structures the day around writing goals. The process of discussing writing goals and achievements is one way of developing understanding of the process and thinking about how to manage it. These discussions are likely to help people negotiate task complexity, in a way that makes time for writing, after a retreat.

The role of the facilitator, at retreat, is always seen as important in holding the boundaries, making writers stick to the designated timeslots, but individuals say they use these timeslots when writing in solitude too, after a retreat.

The experience of containment at retreat enables participants to develop self-containment in other settings. This is not to say that every participant now writes every day and overcomes every barrier to writing; containment is a dynamic process. There will still be times when there is conflict between tasks and roles, but self-containment, developed over time, will help in negotiating it.

The key is to develop holistic self-containment: emotional, organisational and epistemological self-containment. If we have only one or two of these dimensions, we may not have self-containment, and we may not write as much as we want to, or we may not write what we want to. This may be why it is easier to develop self-containment with others who have experienced holistic containment: they know the value of writing in containing settings, and they know what the components of containment are. They have begun to process and practice writing in containing settings. They are prepared to co-construct containing sessions with other writers, because they know that this will mean that they can write. In addition, some of them create containing settings for others, for students who are starting work on dissertations, for example.

Strategic engagement

As a result of our studies (MacLeod *et al.* 2012), we have developed the concept of strategic engagement to describe this dynamic approach to managing multiple tasks.

Structured writing retreats allow participants to develop and practice strategic engagement and integrate potentially fragmenting or competing roles. This explains how we can construct the writing role in a range of environments. It explains our role not as a series of strands (Åkerlind 2005), but as a series of strategic engagements.

This means that writing may be the primary task without displacing all our other tasks. It also means that there will be less anxiety during periods when we are not writing. If we designate periods when other tasks have primacy – knowing that there will be times when writing has primacy – we know we will progress our writing, and we can focus on other primary tasks.

The experience of making writing the primary task can suggest new ways of writing and new ways of managing competing tasks. The experience of making writing the primary task may be a precondition for strategic engagement.

Finally, the writing meeting template (Appendix G) described in Chapter 6 works well at end of a retreat to generate containment beyond it. It also creates opportunities for discussing options: in writing meetings writers can review and set up other containing environments. In this way, the writing meeting template can be used to manage strategic engagement in writing.

Conclusion

> Writing in a group removes the associated self-pity I often experience, which in itself acts as a writer's block. It changes my emotions associated with the task from being negative to more positive ones.

Containment theory explains some of the problems with writing, and holistic containment offers some solutions. This theory explains how social writing contains negative emotions associated with writing. It also explains how social writing can reduce the stress that writing often brings.

More importantly, containment theory explains how it is that social writing works as a multifaceted framework for writing. Within the apparently simple act of sitting down to write together, all the facets of containment are brought into play: emotional, organisational and epistemological. This is not to say that any group, setting out to do any writing, will provide all of these forms of containment; it may be important to deploy structures and processes for social writing described in earlier chapters. But using containment theory in this way has shown how to confront difficulties we have with writing – not just to see them as our individual difficulties – and to start addressing them.

Containment theory explains why we can solve some of these problems so quickly in social writing, although this may create the illusion that writing 'problems' are easily resolved. Perhaps some will see this as proof of the myth that anyone who has problems with writing should be doing something else. Similarly, when we read accounts of experiences of structured writing retreats, we could read them as evidence of the need for writing development, or we could interpret them as containment-in-action, since many of their comments combine the three components of containment.

To illustrate this, here are responses collected at a fifteen-minute, end-of-retreat discussion with twelve participants (including myself):

1   Excellent feedback from others – important that you can act on the feedback right away at retreat. We're all in the same frame of mind and focusing on writing.
2   It shows you what's possible. When I arrived I didn't know what to expect, but now I know how to make this work.
3   It's made the intangible tangible.
4   People's comments tell you that what you're doing is worthwhile.
5   It's not just the words you're saying, but the fact that you're saying it aloud. You lose the fear.
6   There are no distractions. No other roles to play. You don't have to think about anything else, and this frees up your mind to focus on your writing.
7   Deliberately not checking emails at retreat is part of this. Longest period of time that I've been off the internet.
8   Social media – being embedded in that world – important to be able to come in and out of it. Find its place in my work. Using tweet to sum up what I've done in the past three hours' writing, for example.

9   If I don't answer students' emails at the weekends I feel guilty, but I did not feel that here, which is a better way of working and more healthy. It's not about abstinence; it's about managing it.

10 Another lovely group of colleagues.

11 Coming back to my second retreat is very different – very different from the first time. Less anxious. Feel more relaxed and more in control. Feel I got more out of it. Understand how to use the time slots.

12 Do you work towards the next retreat – people who have been to several? Yes. It's a way of setting goals.

13 This is why the on-campus retreat days work so well.

14 Also deals with anxiety of other writing environments – now I think about retreat in relation to this experience, which is positive and productive.

15 It makes getting started with writing task less intimidating.

16 Helps me to stop hiding behind reading – which means I don't write. I said at the start I've not prepared enough – I can't write for the whole day. But I did. I remembered the authors I wanted to write about, and could write about them and fill in details of dates etc. later.

17 I used to bring bags of books to retreat, and I'm now down to one bag. So managed to take away the layers.

18 Relief. Absolute relief. No guilt about not communicating with your work. To come away for a weekend . . . work is constantly on your mind, your head's full of it. You plan not to answer emails at the weekend, but you always do. But not here. Less feeling of inadequacy. Great feeling in the evening that I've done enough, so I do take a break. Also morning and afternoon breaks and breaks for lunch – good to switch off, quickly, because you know you'll be going back to it. It's a positive structure. It's head space. Also having permission to talk about your research.

19 Mixture of nationalities, disciplines, backgrounds, experiences and stories is very interesting. All working on same wavelength. Supportive. Not competitive.

20 Structure of the days: I usually do multiple tasks at the same time, but will change that now, focusing on one thing at a time. Less stressful and more productive.

21 Also that we don't need a ten-hour day. That you can just feel happy with writing for thirty minutes. And be productive that way.

22 When I read the retreat programme, I wondered why we have to work so little, but in reality structuring the day in this way you are more effective than doing much longer slots, especially when you are writing at home, you are continually doing other things.

At first glance, these comments seem like the usual collection of confidence boosting and group support that most people get from most experiences of social writing, but if we apply containment theory we can learn more about these writers' experiences. Their comments illustrate the experience of containment:

they explicitly refer to managing (containing) the unmanageable (uncontainable). There is evidence of emotional containment – unmanageable feelings became manageable; organisational containment – they developed practices that contributed to professional clarity; and there are signs of epistemological containment – they discussed and made sense of uncertainties or complexities in their work. It's all there.

More specifically, the first and fourth comments suggest that writing with others clarified meaning, process and role. This suggests that the 'all in the same boat' comment that comes up so often should not simply be read as a feature of a therapeutic support group but as a sign of the emerging clarity – they can now see that writing is part of what they do. Of course, they knew beforehand that writing was a key part of their jobs, but it had never before been the primary task.

Comments two and three explicitly define the process of making the unmanageable manageable. Comment five – 'You lose the fear' – explicitly conveys emotional containment, as do comments about developing 'positive' feelings about writing and finding ways to make writing 'less intimidating'. It is clear from a couple of comments that they made writing the primary task: 'There are no distractions. No other roles to play. You don't have to think about anything else, and this frees up your mind to focus on your writing' (comment six).

They managed competing tasks and were thinking about ways of managing these tasks in other settings: 'If I don't answer students' emails at the weekends I feel guilty, but I did not feel that here, which is a better way of working and more healthy. It's not about abstinence; it's about managing it' (comment nine).

This one group's views should not be seen as a random collection of thoughts – particularly since this list is representative of end-of-retreat discussions – but as evidence of containment. This is not just positive feedback – although is there any reason why people who are writing should not also be happy? – but evidence of the more complex processes going on, on several levels. This is not to say that everyone experiences every form of containment at every retreat – we do not yet have data on that, either way – but there is a possibility that they did.

Moreover, as more and more people attend these retreats, experience these processes and adopt these perspectives, perhaps there will be some impact on an organisational level. In the meantime, they already construct organisational containment in microcosm, in micro-groups, and there is evidence that this is transferred to workplace settings.

The paradox that writing can be deeply problematic, but that the 'problem' of writing can be quickly and easily solved in containing social settings points to the power not only of social processes to boost our writing but also of other settings to disrupt it. For every retreat, there may be someone who questions why we 'need' retreats. For every retreat participant, there may be twice as many people who are afraid to 'confront their demons', since facing up to our own goals and setting out to achieve them is not always comfortable. It can be painful. Many are afraid, and some cloak their fear in critique. There may be active resistance to the concept of containment, which might signal an unwillingness to buy into the model of social writing. It may be difficult immediately to find others who co-commit to this way of writing.

As long as social writing remains in the margins of academic and professional work it can be positioned as remedial or developmental, meriting short-term funding, seeking quick solutions to the 'problem' of writing and quick returns on this 'investment'. To complicate matters further, none of these issues is routinely discussed in academic and professional workplaces.

Social writing – in any form – provides opportunities for everyone to discuss the problem of writing and negotiate their way around the contested space that writing occupies in our professional and, often, personal lives. We should now begin to think of social writing as the construction of a healthy organisational culture.

The components of social writing involved in containment are:

- acknowledging the role of containment in developing a healthy organisational culture that facilitates writing;
- constructing holistic containment in discussions with others who want to write; and
- developing self-containment through these collective activities.

It is not enough simply to look for more time, or try to make more time for writing. If emotions associated with writing are uncontained, we are just as unlikely to write when we have more time (Boice 1987a). In any case, how likely is it that the institutions in which we work will present us with more time for writing? We need to integrate writing in the rest of our work and the rest of our lives.

This chapter identified some of the factors – conscious and unconscious, institutional and individual – that may prevent us from making time and space to write. It applied containment theory to deepen our understanding of these factors and construct a set of concepts, behaviours and relationships to help us to manage these factors.

The next chapter explores the implications of this theory and these practices for those with leadership roles. It explains the leadership role in social writing. While many social writing groups have no formal leader, there is evidence that a certain type of leadership makes social writing work.

Chapter 9

Leadership

Because so many so people tell me that leadership is critical for social writing, this chapter focuses on that role. Participants say that the effect of social writing relies on someone holding them to the social writing model. Otherwise, discussions run over time or people don't start writing, and that cuts into writing time.

Leadership in this context involves creating clarity about and focus on the primary task of writing. It involves acknowledging that writing may not be the primary task in other environments. It involves creating a space where the negotiation between competing tasks may take place.

Defining leadership for social writing also means acknowledging that leadership means developing other people's skills, and in social writing this includes facilitating discussions of writing. It is in these discussions that people learn the specifics of writing practice – which can feel like learning the 'code' of writing – and they can learn different ways of writing. Social writing leadership, therefore, is about facilitating discussions of writing, while making writing the primary task.

This is why containment theory is useful for exploring this leadership role: while the previous chapter used containment theory to develop our understanding of how one form of social writing can enable writing, this chapter uses containment theory to explore the role of the person who leads – or facilitates – social writing. The previous chapter explained how a structured writing retreat works to contain writing-related anxieties, makes writing the primary task and prevents anti-task behaviours. This chapter explores the leadership role and explores how it is implicated in these effects. It draws on a study (Murray *et al.* 2012) of the leadership role in structured writing retreats (see Chapter 5) and proposes that this role may be applied in similar ways, with similar effects, in other forms of social writing.

By 'leadership' I mean neither formal leadership nor a managerialist model (Deem 1998, 2005) but something more like a 'contingent, relational and negotiated reality' of leadership (Middlehurst 2008: 337). While Middlehurst was writing about higher education, I propose that this view has relevance for writing in many settings. In fact, each context will have its own contingencies and relationships, requiring its own negotiations; it is these contingencies and relationships that create the need for a relational model of writing. This links the concept of leadership much more closely to the performance of writing.

Yes, of course academics, researchers and professionals will have the skills for both solitary and social writing. Nevertheless, the ability to perform these skills regularly, on demand and in relation to other tasks, may benefit from leadership, even if leadership rotates among participating writers, as is often the case in social writing.

This chapter explores this leadership role and makes the case for different ways of playing it in different groups. This chapter is not about institutionally defined leadership, but informal leadership that different people can perform in different social writing settings. This discussion will explain how different group members can take on this role.

This type of leadership involves applying the principles described throughout this book, buying into one or more of the models proposed, and holding the writing group to these models. This can seem like 'forcing' writing and writers, but that does seem to be an important part of the role. This role is particularly important for those who are still learning to use social writing practices, but it also seems to be useful for those who are more experienced in social writing. In both cases the leader helps participants to develop and maintain writing-oriented relationships.

'Leadership' may not be the best word for this, because of its associations with formal roles. 'Facilitator' may be a better word to describe this negotiated role. However, while both terms are used in this chapter, leadership is its title because it does seem to be important to have someone take responsibility for holding the group to social writing. It does seem to be important to have someone 'leading' in that sense.

Key messages

- It is important to have someone act as leader in social writing – to hold the boundaries, time limits, behaviours and focus on writing activities, conversations and relationships.
- This involves informal leadership, often rotating in a group.
- The leader's role is to manage social writing (rather than provide writing instruction, mentoring or coaching).
- They hold participants to the values and structures of social writing.

There are examples of social writing that incorporate a mentoring role, which has been defined as a leadership strategy (Jackson 2009: 10). That model used a 'servant leadership' model, adopting principles of leadership: mentoring, coaching and peer learning. There are initiatives for creating research communities (Murray 2012a; Ng and Pemberton 2013).

However, it may seem that focusing on writing in the ways described in this book is to miss the point: should we not be developing research rather than just 'writing'? How can new researchers write, if they have nothing to write about? Surely 'leadership' is about helping people develop in other ways, through training in research methods, for example?

My answer to these questions is to give writing a central role in researcher development and research activity. From the start, both in my work and in this book, I have assumed that writing develops thinking, ideas, personal interests, motivation, relevant research skills and networks. It is not just about getting words down on paper; we can write when we are not sure what we think or what we want to do, and we can develop our thinking by writing at this stage and at each stage in the research process.

The role of social writing leaders, therefore, is about creating research cultures where these developmental activities may occur, acknowledging that these activities are part of the research process.

The impulse to develop a research community may be triggered by 'a desire to improve and develop the research prowess of the collective members' (Ng and Pemberton 2013: 1536). The impulse to do social writing may be triggered by a desire to increase written outputs and research income. However, it has been argued that such communities 'reflect the individual's need for additional support and social interaction' (Ng and Pemberton 2013: 1536). What starts out as research development may become a social group.

However this book focuses on writing-oriented relationships, and how these develop research activities and outputs. These relationships do not depend on a 'leader', but they do depend on someone creating a space where these relationships can develop. This space and these relationships are even more important in the broader context of competitive writing and research.

Even when it is not absolutely clear to participants how they might develop these relationships it is important to have someone who will hold the model, so that participants can experience it for themselves and decide whether or not it will work for them and whether or not they can write with the people who have turned up for a particular social writing meeting, or whether will have to look outside their departments for other social writers. In that instance, once they have seen what social writing leadership involves, they may take on the leadership role themselves.

Leadership in social writing

> The writing is not valued. The publication of it is ticked off against your record, but the actual process of it is not supported very well.

This quotation from one of the many interviews (in a British Academy-funded study) shows the problem this chapter addresses. Leadership in relation to writing is experienced by many solely as the setting and monitoring of targets; it is not seen as supporting the achievement of these targets, either in the sense of learning how to achieve them or in the sense of managing competing tasks to as to achieve them.

The leadership role in social writing involves five main functions (Murray *et al.* 2012: 767):

1   Briefing participants, explaining the rationale for the structure (of the retreat, workshop, group etc.), describing the schedule and suggesting ways of making social writing work;
2   Prompting participants to set writing goals, align them with scheduled writing sessions and discuss goals and achievements;
3   Prompting further discussion of goals and achievements during breaks from writing;
4   Holding a fixed programme of writing and discussions sessions;
5   Modelling the writing process in the group.

This form of leadership provides emotional, organisational and epistemological containment (defined in the previous chapter). This allows participants – and the facilitator – to focus on writing.

Emotional containment is provided by the leader setting a positive tone for social writing, being supportive, encouraging and helpful, while also 'cracking the whip' in a way that is experienced as 'keeping people on track':

> I think having a facilitator who is very focused . . . is absolutely essential . . . [it is] very much the leadership. You need someone who is sympathetic, who is focused themselves and who you can turn to, who you can ask questions, but who won't be sidetracked.

It seems to be important for the leader to also be a participant in social writing, modelling both writing and collegiality:

> The retreat leader wrote alongside you, and I think that made a huge difference, because she wasn't saying, 'Right, I'll be back in an hour'. She sat there the whole time, and she was writing alongside as a colleague, and that really made a difference, and also you knew that [she] had major publications. It gives her credibility.

This type of leadership might, therefore, involve simply setting the tone, or, with a more experienced leader, providing support or coaching in research or writing.

However, we should remember that it is not only the leader who creates these effects; it is the containing structure of social writing that creates them, and the leader simply holds participants to that structure. Relationships among participants are also implicated in the impact of social writing.

Organisational containment is provided by social writing, in terms of its structure, the leader's ability to hold participants to it and the ability to convey the expectation that clarity and focus will emerge through social writing. This is often conveyed in uses of the word 'discipline':

[The facilitator] kept us on task and provided a kind of discipline in the sense that sessions started at a certain time, and unlike unsupervised writing it wasn't possible to say, 'I've had enough'. So it meant that for two hours there was nothing else to do other than write.

Of course, not everyone will like having a leader who does this for/to them:

Given the structure of the programme, there had to be somebody there to say, here is what we are doing. Start now. Finish now. But that was alien to me . . . that experience of somebody setting the scene and then saying, 'Right, it's time to start', and . . . 'Everybody stop talking and get down to the writing task'. And that I didn't enjoy.

Perhaps some do not want or require containment. Perhaps some will not see its value. Or is it, instead, that this way of writing is more than likely to be 'alien', at first, to those who have never used social writing or never heard of it before, but quickly becomes more comfortable?

I found the whole thing quite horrific when I heard about it . . . I thought that just sounds to me like the typing pool from hell, and it was nothing like that in actual fact.

What about those of us – perhaps most of us – for whom there is no precedent for social writing, and where there is no history of it in our studying or working environments? Will the facilitator have to find some way of helping people to overcome these reservations, to persuade them to give social writing a try? Does the leader have to persist in finding people to write with, whether or not he or she continues to be the leader of the group that forms? Will leaders talking about their own reservations about social writing help? This is not to say that people will or should become dependent on social writing leaders, or that leaders will become dependent on writing groups; in fact, the opposite often happens, as writers develop self-containment.

Epistemological containment is provided by leaders who help participants think through and make sense of their writing projects. This may include providing feedback on writing-in-progress. The value of social writing is that it provides 'synchronous peer review' (Murray and Newton 2009: 546) and, unlike other feedback processes, it means that writers can immediately act on such feedback in their next writing slot, if they choose to do so. The facilitator is not, however, the provider of all feedback, but encourages mutual peer review of writing processes and practices, not just of texts.

Holistic containment occurs when all three of the above forms of containment – emotional, organisational and epistemological – are experienced. In social writing settings, like a structured writing retreat, these three elements were not only experienced by participants, but were integrated in that social writing environment.

While social writing involves the active participation of all members of the group, there is a strong sense among participants that the leadership role is key to this effect.

Social writing leaders do not have to be in a formal leadership role; they have to be willing to lead the group. This is not about assuming a leadership function through informal channels. In fact, it is not necessary to have the same person play the leadership role at all social writing meetings; people can take turns – as long as someone performs the five functions listed above.

Social writing leaders do not have to be writing experts. They do not have to be the most published people in the room. What they have to be able to do – what they have to want to do – is make writing the focus. That is what provides containment – containing leadership involves holding participants, and oneself, to one of the social writing formats.

One of the most difficult tasks for the social writing leader is interrupting discussions and stopping people writing. When the time a group has allocated for writing is up – a ninety-minute slot, for example – the leader has to ask people to stop writing, whether they feel like stopping or not. Likewise, the leader has to interrupt the brief planning and stock-taking conversations – which may be extremely interesting – in order to get people to start writing. This may be the leader's most important role; if the time limits are not imposed, conversations will continue, and writing time will be lost. The leader has to be there to stop anything impinging on the act of writing.

This may feel disruptive, for both participants and the leader, who is also writing, after all. The group has to agree that these interruptions are not about ignoring people's contributions. This is not about suppressing people's talk. It is about holding each other to the model in order to write. In fact, the experience of discomfort at these interruptions may signal the need for strategic engagement.

Strategic engagement

It is all very well providing containing leadership at writing retreats, but how can containing leadership be performed in other settings – in the workplace or at home? Participants suggest that such leadership is not provided for writing in their workplaces. This creates a distinct contrast – and potential tensions – between containing social writing environments and normal working environments. Ideally, it would be good to have a bridge between the two or at least to have some way to reduce this tension. Developing a strategy for managing this conflict is an important part of the writing process.

Strategic engagement is a concept developed to explain how this conflict might be managed (Murray *et al.* 2012). In social writing we can develop our ability to manage this conflict. This may be because social writing gives us opportunities to enact this skill and develop this ability. The ability to start and stop writing at specific predetermined times may be central to this ability, and the role of the leader in enforcing these time limits may be central to our ability to manage the conflict between writing and other tasks. Thereby, we may achieve the clarity that is so important for our writing and thinking but that we know we cannot achieve, to the same extent, in many other environments.

The process of stopping and starting writing at predetermined times is a mechanism of strategic engagement, in the sense that it involves imposing this strategy on our engagement with writing. This makes it possible to learn how to disengage from other tasks in order to write (see Chapter 7). It can feel uncomfortable. It can feel like being pulled away from the task you would rather be doing, in order to write. It can feel like being pulled away from writing just when you were on a roll or in the 'flow' of writing:

Participant's feedback at the end of her first retreat (December 2013)

> The structure: what worked really well for me was . . . I wasn't sure I would fit into the structure, because I like to keep going if it's working, but I found that stopping while you're in the middle of something, you knew where you were going with it and could get back into it quickly. Previously, I would just keep writing, but it would have taken me much longer to get back into it after a break, which is probably why I don't dare take regular breaks while writing, but this way is much more productive and much healthier.

Unsolicited email from the same participant, one month later

> I was one of the folk at the writing retreat in early December. I shared at the end of the retreat that I had been feeling rather concerned prior to attending – that I would find it disruptive to be interrupted when 'in a flow' and to my surprise that what I found was that it made re-engaging with writing much easier. Previous to the workshop my usual approach was to keep working until I finished a section if I was 'in a flow' and then I would find it quite a thought to start writing again and procrastinate and be rather unproductive and frustrated with myself.
>
> I have been making a point of leaving my writing at a good point, by which I mean I know where I'm going with it, and I am really pleased that I continue to find it easier to re-engage as a result.
>
> For the first time – today – I actually felt that I was looking forward to writing and hence my decision to email you and share this. So thanks again.

This shows that the writer has been able to write on her own – that may sound absurd. Of course, she is able to write on her own, but she has now learned a new strategy that will make it easier to start writing and has already, in just one month, made writing less daunting.

The social writing leader, who played the containing role at the writing retreat she attended, was not there when she continued with the writing she describes in the second quote. This suggests that she is developing the ability to provide containment for her writing. She is managing competing tasks – a key component of productive writing. This example also shows that this change in practice may not take all that long to develop.

Strategic engagement is therefore a way of explaining the process of starting to write before you feel ready and stopping writing before you feel ready. This means that writing does not impinge on other tasks; nor does it place writing in a simple, but unhelpful, dichotomy with other tasks. Strategic engagement is the ability to identify, prioritise and perform a specific primary task at a specific time and to move between primary tasks. Supporting strategic engagements is therefore a key function of leadership.

Growing communities of writers

> People-related problems arise from self-doubt, especially for those with academic capital under pressure to be research active in the quest for scientific capital and career progression. Such problems can also be compounded where faculty support is limited and the nature of the work 'isolating', where there are research cliques or where there is a perceived absence of collegiality.
>
> (Holligan *et al.* 2011: 726)

This commentary helpfully points to links between 'self-doubt', 'the nature of the work' and social cultures. That it is not all about the individual is a helpful reminder in times when the unit of assessment in writing is often exactly that – the individual. These authors also raise the role of 'capital' in research development and go some way towards defining the different forms of capital that might be implicated in research development and activity. Finally, the role of 'collegiality' is a theme in discussions of research cultures, but could constructing collegialities not be an active process for those who face these problems?

Having established the principles of social writing, and its benefits, and having defined the leadership role, we can create communities that make it possible to write. This is not so much about coaching writers – although there is an extensive and impressive literature on that (Geller and Eodice 2013) – but about leading the social writing activity. This relates to recent writing on collegial models of research leadership and research capacity development (Biesta *et al.* 2011; Boice 1992; Christie and Menter 2009; Holligan *et al.* 2011; Murray and Pollard 2011; Nagy 2011; Nutley *et al.* 2003; Powell and Orme 2011; Sharland 2012). While much of this research is located in the social sciences, I propose that it has relevance for other disciplines, and my experience of working with multidisciplinary groups confirms this.

While we might not all agree that collegiality is the answer, or even that lack of it is the problem, we can surely see the importance of context and relationships in how we work, and in how we think and feel about our work. For some, this will seem like no more than navel-gazing; to others, it will seem to deny individual agency. I do not want to argue either of these extremes. Instead, I am trying to map out interrelationships between the individuals and their contexts, with an emphasis on 'social' elements, but this is primarily because they are so often neglected or denied. Hence this book.

Perhaps we should see developing as a writer as a process of growing, facilitating and 'being facilitated' as a writer in many communities – not just one. (See the section on micro-groups in Chapter 5.) In this way, social writing can serve as an apprenticeship in writing. While there is an unspoken assumption that writing involves sitting alone in an office for many hours until the writing is completed, this is unrealistic in today's working environments, particularly where there is 'dis-integration', supercomplexity or fragmentation (Barnett 1999; Åkerlind 2005; Clegg 2008). The solitary writing model is not available and, in any case, it does not work for everyone.

Social writing is about engaging in discourse about what we do when we write. It also involves recovering the social in writing in the sense of defining writing as a social act, an act that is socially constructed and socially performed. Social writing leadership is about holding the space and time dedicated to that understanding of writing.

This brings collective gains, as the generation of ideas becomes part of everyone's experience. The benefits of social writing are not just for those who succeed in publishing or winning grants. Participants are actively involved in the process of generating not only ideas and knowledge but also collective practices that, in turn, will stimulate further production of ideas and knowledge. Leaders and participants in social writing will be those who buy into this concept, who can see or imagine value – even 'value-added' – in the work of such communities.

Becoming a social writing leader

> When these spaces are provided, individuals are supported to perform informal leadership, as groupings of academics [and others] meet to support each other's writing.
>
> (Murray *et al.* 2012: 776)

In this context 'leadership' does not necessarily involve developing special 'leader-like' qualities or competencies. It means using social writing strategies and helping the group stick with them for long enough to develop their writing practices and, perhaps, their confidence in their ability to write. It means holding to the time limits, using goal setting and monitoring, using writing warm ups, discussing writing goals and meeting to write regularly with others. In this way, both leaders and participants will develop an understanding of writing – and of the pressure and anxieties it brings, not in terms of individual shortcomings but as social or environmental factors, and this will provide clarity and focus in writing. If we accept that writing is shaped by social and environmental factors, we should surely actively engage social processes in our writing.

Once writers have adopted these strategies and made them their own, they are able to do social writing in a range of ways and with a range of people. Some will take on the role of leader. This means that on return to working environments where writing is generally not privileged, they will be able to prevent other tasks impinging on writing and will be able to write.

Novice social writing leaders may have uncertainties about taking on this role and may also have anxieties about their own writing. It may be a good idea to start by working with participants who are willing to try these strategies, rather than those who are itching to demolish them. In any case, this is a light touch form of leadership, which often does not feel like leading at all, although some will find the interruptions to their conversations and the injunctions to start and stop writing 'alien'. With any social writing group, the leader has to be able to persevere. Leaders and writers will surely learn from playing the various roles in social writing settings. In this way, leadership can grow from within the group and among participants in the group.

This argument may be even more valid at a time when, and in environments where, many forms leadership are operating at the same time – formal, informal, distributed, hierarchical, relational, managerial and hybrid. In these settings, 'positional power' may be less important (Middlehurst 2008: 332) than other forms of power. Moreover, it may be that leadership is relational in the sense that it emerges from relationships between people (Bolden *et al.* 2008). Writing leadership may emerge from relationships between writers. Creating relationships and having interactions around writing is one way of sustaining writing and thereby sustaining research and other activities. Supporting these relationships and interactions is therefore a key component of research leadership.

The great advantage of taking on the leadership role in social writing is knowing that you will have time to write – that's what's in it for leaders. There is also encouragement to be had in the knowledge that everyone in the room shares a common goal – they are all committed to writing. There is therefore a link between what individuals want to do and what the leader wants to do. This common goal is the basis for collegiality.

Conclusion

> In contexts where definitions of 'strategic' and 'primary' are not fixed, research leadership involves supporting academics [and others] as they negotiate priorities and strategically define the primary task.
>
> (Murray *et al.* 2012: 776)

In studies of social writing interviewees tell us that the leader helps participants manage unmanageable emotions related to writing (emotional containment), provides structure and expectations (organisational containment) and helps participants make sense of their writing projects (epistemological containment). Taken together, these functions help them to make sense of their writing more generally, in relation to their other professional or academic roles (holistic containment).

However, there are so many forms of social writing, and, I assume, so many types of leadership, that it seems more important to talk about leadership in terms of a commitment to writing generally and to social writing specifically. There is likely to be social writing leadership capability among writers and among those who want to write.

The components of social writing involved in leadership are:

- a containing environment: holding boundaries, time limits, behaviours and focus on writing;
- writing-oriented discussions and relationships;
- writing – 'leaders' writing with others; and
- others take on this leadership role.

This chapter moves the argument on from an earlier study of social writing (Murray *et al.* 2012), which concluded that there were implications for leaders in academic and professional settings: they might have to change how they perform their leadership role in relation to writing. Instead, this chapter suggests that there may be writing leaders in many places, at many levels in various organisations. They key is finding those who want to lead in this way, rather than changing formal leadership practices.

This is not to say that those in formal leadership roles will no longer be required to provide containment; clearly, it will still be of benefit if they do. If they can do this in relation to writing, then that will help enormously. More importantly, they can support social writing activities, thereby enabling colleagues to benefit from their containing influence: 'Research leaders can, and should, therefore, be instrumental in the containing effect: at the very least, they can be clear and congruent in their messages about the place of writing for publication within the wider academic role' (Murray *et al.* 2012: 776).

The article from which the above quotation is taken argued that individual academics and professionals were not to be expected to provide containment, but this chapter considered that very option: can those who want to write construct containing environments? Our article listed specific ways in which formal leaders could provide containment, while this chapter explained what writers can do to create containment. Ideally, perhaps there will be both, and both will mutually support each other. Otherwise, there might be a limit to the extent to which individuals can maintain emotional and epistemological containment in organisations that lack organisational containment.

While there may indeed be identifiable, recognisable characteristics of social writing leadership, we should perhaps look to those who want to write, to see if they can play this leadership role. Leadership in this sense does not require expertise either in writing or in leadership, but a commitment to social writing practices.

There are, potentially, many different ways of performing the social writing leader's role.

Social writing leadership roles

- Getting a group together and holding the structure
- taking turns to chair a writing group
- sharing leadership of micro-groups
- discussing writing practices with new writers
- discussing social writing with other writers and leaders.

This chapter has focused on what many participants say is the key component of social writing – leadership. It has explained what that role involves, and how different people can play the role in different ways, in different groupings. The main argument has been that this is not formal leadership but informal, relational leadership.

The next chapter pulls all of the previous chapters together. It argues that all of the components described in earlier chapters, taken together, constitute social writing and that, in spite of its many variations, there is a core set of principles that make it work. It also provides a model of social writing that holds these principles together.

Chapter 10

A framework for social writing

The Social Writing Framework

> [Writing] requires me to bring all my attention and energy to bear on the tasks that it involves (thinking, formulating, experimenting, drafting, reflecting, reading, synthesising, generating ideas, pulling together a lot of information, drawing out key themes, articulating complex ideas, adopting positions, generating explanations, reaching conclusions etc.).

This describes the complexity of writing. For such a complex task we need a complex model. It must encapsulate the many components of writing discussed in previous chapters, and it should accommodate the many processes involved. A complex model of writing should also include relationships with other people, places and things that constitute social writing environments. In addition, since writing is implicated in many other activities, there must be containment of writing and other activities.

The Social Framework is one way of explaining how we can do this. It can be used to construct social writing concepts and practices. It incorporates all the features that positively influence writing behaviours and outcomes.

It may also have explanatory power: it may account for the impact of a specific writing practice on productivity. It may explain why people who intend to write fail to do so. It is not possible to say how many of the framework's components need to be missing for writing to fail, but this framework could help those who want to write, but cannot, analyse their practices to see if there are components that they should add.

The framework has two elements: the inner circle contains the cognitive, social and physical components of social writing, and the smaller circles surrounding them represent the components of social writing. This arrangement is not intended to suggests links to areas within the circle, because interrelationships between them are too various to be represented in that way.

It might seem odd to have a 'social' component in a 'social' framework, but this is to signify that while the whole framework depends on interactions and relationships, these will occur in conversations with other writers. Without this component, there would likely be conversations about written outputs rather

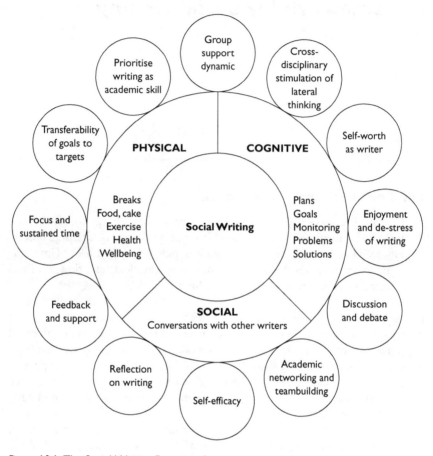

Figure 10.1 The Social Writing Framework

than practices. The whole framework therefore depicts a general social environment, while the social segment depicts a specific social activity.

It may seem mundane to include 'goals' and 'targets'. It may seem trivial to include food and, specifically, cake in a framework for academic writing. It may seem irrelevant to bring exercise and going for a walk into this context. It may seem transgressive to give as much space to 'self-efficacy' as to 'academic networking'.

Some sectors are notorious for the lavish hospitality provided at training events and professional meetings, but perhaps we would not choose them as role models. We are much less likely to talk about how much better we felt after swim, how much cake we ate at a retreat or how beautiful the mountains looked when the sun hit the snow on return to work, for fear of social writing being seen as a junket. Our health and wellbeing, physical and mental, matter to our employers, but providing us with good food and access to exercise facilities are not what they might see as their core business. Yet these are crucial to the impact of retreats. Not only are these components included in this model, but there are details of each of them throughout this book.

It is important to adopt some of the hospitality ethic or ethic of care for people who are writing. It does help to be well looked after, to know that you are being looked after at writing retreats. It does aid concentration, not to have to think about making meals, for example, but to focus exclusively on writing. It is experienced as part of the positive impact of social writing that there is a collaborative and collegial ethos – this comes up in all the feedback sessions – and this is a welcome change from the normally competitive environments where people work. Even in environments that are not competitive, writing is often in competition with other tasks for primacy.

This framework 'outs' the writing process – as a social process. It defines the many types of processes that constitute writing as a social process. It shows how writing consists of writing-oriented relationships – relationships with and between many different processes, spaces, people and objects.

The positive outcome of practising writing as a social process is that people feel there is a place for them, a role for them, as academic writers. It provides a way of constructing writing as part of being a scholar, of taking up that position and acting it out.

This is not as circumscribed as it sounds: conversations about writing, that are part of social writing, are not fixed by any kind of agenda. The framework can stimulate and contain conversations about writing. Using this framework conversations about writing are likely to happen, and writing is likely to happen.

What is particularly appealing about this framework for me is that it unifies the identities of writer, researcher, academic, professional, person, partner, parent, athlete etc. – it does not separate out these roles. Yes, when we go to a writing retreat we leave our jobs, partners and responsibilities behind, but structured writing retreats provide a social setting where conversations create links between the many different components of our lives. The Social Writing Framework shows that it is important to connect exercise and wellbeing with writing; social writing establishes that connection and creates relationships among people who also see, value and practice this and many other connections.

The effect of this is that it feels like all parts of my life relate to my writing. All parts of me are involved in my writing. This effect is sustained in the social writing groups I attend. This is why, for me, when all this talk of the 'social' seems to risk losing sight of the individual, I find that the opposite is true. The individual is, in any case, constructed by his/her social environment, but it is possible to construct a social writing environment for writing. This book offers a range of models for building our own writing societies. We can use these to support emerging researchers, postgraduate students and others who are just beginning to write and publish.

Exposing the workings of academic writing in this way, in this framework, is to some extent exposing the workings of work. This may lead us to question certain ways of working and the ways in which the world of work positions writing. This may, in turn, lead us to continue with an 'inquiry' approach to our writing. It is not that we know all we need to know, since we are learning with each writing project that we are involved in and, potentially, every piece of writing that we do.

Vignettes

> The concept, remaining merely conceptual, falls short of the bite of physical presence. Just one step away is the debilitating idea that a concept is as forceful in its conception as in its realization.
>
> (Truitt 1982: 142)

This section is intended to complement the conceptual content of the Social Writing Framework with vignettes of social writing. These vignettes capture the specifics of social writing. They draw on conversations about writing that occur in breaks and social time, when people are processing what they think is going on in their social writing. They describe their experiences and make sense of the writing strategies they are using. These vignettes describe what they see and what they say. They therefore combine my observations and theirs, including physical details of social writing. The vignettes shed light on how they make sense of their experience through such conversations.

If it seems that this is not relevant to writing, I would emphasise that all these vignettes do relate directly to writing. All of these topics come up in many conversations about writing. They were and are, therefore, literally related to writing by people in the midst of the writing process. Moreover, it seems that all of these components can influence and shape writing practices, which is why we should attend to the components included in the conceptual framework and described in these vignettes when we write.

Vignette 1: Raising mood

As people troop in to writing group meetings they look and sound tired and deflated. They are apologetic – they haven't done as much writing as they wanted to – as much as they said they would last time. They plug in laptops and tell each other their writing goals for this session. They start writing and silence falls. No more talking. There is peace and quiet as they write. After seventy-five minutes' writing they stop and take stock. They enjoyed writing. They feel they've done something worthwhile. As they leave the room they look and sound positive and refreshed.

Vignette 2: Good food

Morning break at a writing retreat means freshly made pancakes with warm maple syrup or scones still warm from the oven with butter, jam and cream. People chat about the writing they've just done, their next writing tasks, difficult stages negotiated or still to come and how good the food is. At the last break on the last day, there is a twelve-inch, two-tier Victoria sponge, decorated with icing, cream and chocolate. Fresh fruit is also available. At the end of each break we wonder if we'll be hungry enough to eat our next meal, but we usually are.

Vignette 3: Collective concentration

Silence falls. We start writing. Everyone's looking at their screen. With a glance at a list, article or book, we carry on typing. For ninety minutes the only sound is clicking keys, the odd cough or noises outside – a dog barks, a bus moves off, a door closes. We don't notice. Aware only of the screen, our thoughts, our writing and each other. We are focused on our writing. This is all we have to do – there is no other task. No internet. No interruptions. We are all in the same boat. Writing together. In silence. Everyone's writing.

Vignette 4: Research networking and exchange

'Have you read that book on doing qualitative research?' 'I can give a copy of the article'. 'I can send you a copy of my ethics form'. 'I had feedback like that once – it's not as bad as it sounds'. 'The reviewer probably had a bad day'. 'I showed my worst review to a [well known] Professor, and she said she gets this kind of thing 50 per cent of the time'. Information exchange, research links, problem solving and collaboration – captured on Post-it notes, so we all see these research connections and solutions. It really feels like a research culture.

Vignette 5: Time out

Time for a break after six hours of writing. In twos and threes we walk round the village, get a newspaper from the shop, listen to the piano playing in the corner house, walk round Gartmore House or 'Wee Wood' circular walk, if there's enough daylight. Or head to the gym or swim. Two or three head to the bar to sit in front on the stove and catch up with the locals. Some have a nap. Some write on – making the most of the time they have here – their time out is dinner.

Vignette 6: Exercise and physical activity

We drive to the gym. Leaving the village, we pass the glade of Douglas firs. The road winds round the loch, inches from the water, and we have our first view of the mountain. We split up – gym or swim. I unwind in the sauna, till the other guests go to dinner and the pool empties, then do twenty or thirty lengths. After sitting writing all day, we feel like we're recovering the use of our legs. We drive back refreshed, invigorated and very clean. We've made progress with our writing, and now we feel great.

Vignette 7: Managing writing stress

The first deadline is long gone. I've had three extensions. Over the past few weeks I've been giving PhD students feedback on their writing – two are in the final stages, doing lots of revisions. I submitted a research proposal and have two other deadlines looming. I haven't read a complex collaborative grant proposal – though I planned to respond last month. I have an ongoing research project that needs to move on soon. Knowing I have two days at writing retreat next week, plus weekly writing groups, is keeping me going. I know I'll get it all done then.

Vignette 8: Celebrations

I ordered champagne. I hear corks popping in the kitchen as we finish our last writing session of the day. I announce to the group: someone passed their viva, someone had a promotion. Applause and smiles all round. There are thanks for support and help with viva preparation. People start comparing viva experiences, and someone's dread is met with offers of help in preparing for their exam. We compare promotion experiences, and someone offers to share their CV and 'case'. We pack up laptops and go to dinner. It's a good way to end the writing day.

Vignette 9: Epiphanies

I had my long awaited thesis light bulb moment following last week's writing retreat. I know exactly the direction I'm heading in and the final structure for the thesis (including dates!) is now in place. I am confident I can work to the schedule I've sent to my supervisors and am getting on with it more quickly and assuredly than before. It's such a relief. I do believe that it was the retreat process and thinking that goes on there that sharpened my mind and, subsequently, my analysis.

Vignette 10: What next?

Time to change gear. Take stock. Sitting with our last dose of coffee and cake, there are pleased and relieved faces around the room, as we tell each other what we achieved. Attention slides to the weekend, the emails, the backlog of everything else. There is a bit of banter about breaking the chains of the retreat structure, but talk turns to how to keep it going. When will we write next? In your office, a café, my home? For ninety minutes, a whole day, an afternoon? We check details of micro-groups and mini-retreats. It's all on the Facebook page.

These vignettes show that it's not all about the writing – or, rather, they show that many processes are involved in writing. These social processes are part of writing. If we cut these from our discussions of writing, from the act of writing or from our conceptualisations of writing, we risk losing part of the writing process and, perhaps more importantly, we will fail to manage or invoke the influence of these processes on/in our writing. Or, we choose to incorporate these processes in our writing practices.

Conclusion

The Social Writing Framework gives us a range of ways of making sense of all the components that may be involved in writing. It is a way of thinking about how we can use these to construct a productive writing process, and how this process may help us to meet imposed writing goals without losing the meaning and value of our writing – for ourselves and for others.

By bringing all these components together in this book, I hope that the workings of writing can be exposed to further scrutiny and analysis by anyone who wants to write. Anyone who writes can use this framework to analyse their writing process. This will mean that writing may be shaped by comprehensive analysis, rather than anecdote and myth. This shaping will help writers to examine what they are doing in more detail, in order to assess how the society in which they write is shaping their writing. In this way, I hope, writing will become social, rather than anti-social.

Conclusion
Concept + experience

The starting point for this book was the assumption that academic writing is relational, in the sense that it constitutes and consists of relationships between scholars, researchers and ideas. These are the ingredients of an intellectual 'society'. This book has described how we can construct intellectual societies for our research and writing. Through social writing we create relationships between ideas and with others who write. This involves building – and/or re-building – relationships between writers and writing.

The ten chapters of this book defined forms of social writing, and each presented a principle of social writing:

1 Writing is not always/only solitary – it's also relational.
2 Writing groups support emerging writerly identities.
3 Talking about writing raises rhetorical awareness.
4 Discussion is part of learning about (and doing) writing.
5 Discussions build writing into research and work.
6 Social writing involves changing writing behaviours.
7 Relationships in research and work develop around writing.
8 Social writing facilitates management of competing tasks.
9 Writing leaders hold the practice of social writing.
10 All these social activities and relationships constitute writing.

Writing is not, therefore, always about the individual expression of ideas in isolation. It need not always and forever be a solitary act. Making writing relational involves creating activities and relationships around writing, in the act of writing. In this way, writing can be open, acknowledged and nurtured. This approach can inject meaning, pleasure and satisfaction into the act of writing. More importantly, it can counteract the risks of solitary writing:

> Never, ever, get yourself into a situation where you have nothing to do but write and read. You'll go into a depression. You have to be doing something good for the world, something undeniably useful; you need exercise, too, *and people.*
>
> (Dillard: xii [my emphasis] in Gutkind 2005: xii)

Dillard might well have been taking about my Social Writing Framework, developed to counter the negative side effects of solitary writing that she warns us about. This solely solitary way of writing does not, of course, necessarily produce depression, but it does have its risks. In any case, even those who believe they can only write in solitude – but do not manage to write as much as they would like – should surely consider alternatives.

It is not always possible to persuade someone to try a new approach, when it seems so uncomfortable or counter-intuitive. However, when I first started to run writer's groups it seemed strange to me too. I was not sure it would work either. I knew there would be people with issues about writing, about groups, about institutional expectations and perhaps about me.

It was not obvious to me at that time that writing in a group would work for me or for anyone else. So I can relate to the doubts that some have about social writing, and I accept that issues with the concept may be barriers to the experience. I get that. We could have the conceptual argument all day, but the experience would give us more to talk about.

This is not to say that everyone who tries social writing will be converted, but without trying it all we have is the concept, and social writing is much, much more than a concept.

Appendix
Programmes and templates

Appendix A: Setting up writer's groups

Introduction

Types of group: writing at meetings, peer review, virtual, face-to-face.
Interdisciplinary/departmental.
Timing: 90-minute meetings every two weeks.

Underpinning principles

- Writing is a social act that benefits from discussion with peers.
- Feedback on text and process can be useful at different stages.
- Working in a group can motivate writers to initiate/progress projects.
- Goal setting and monitoring help writers create and stick to deadlines.

Programme for 90-minute writer's group meeting

5 minutes	Writing in sentences, private writing on the question, 'What writing for the project you are working on have you done, and what do you want to do in the long, medium and short term?' Make goals specific – specify numbers of dates, hours, weeks, words etc.
10 minutes	Discussion in twos, five minutes on each writing project.
70 minutes	Writing.
5 minutes	Taking stock and setting new goal.

Experiences of writing groups

(1) 'You feel as though you and those around you are engaged in the same endeavour. This makes it a bit easier to feel as though what you are doing has meaning and is mutually beneficial'. (2) 'The structure of the group acts as a physical barrier to distractions. Sticking with the writing process, not being distracted,

not checking emails, not looking up references on the internet are all part of the process of writing in a group'.

Prompts for generating text

Warm-up prompt, generic prompts, journal prompts.

Defining writing goals, sub-goals and sub-sub-goals

Content, length of text, purpose of text, number of minutes for writing.

Checklist for starting a writer's group:

- Invent your own set of principles.
- Agree purpose and format. Agree to quit email and internet.
- Initiate common activity: describe your writing projects to each other.
- Have someone act as facilitator to keep to time limits.
- Discuss writing-in-progress. Set specific writing goals.
- Don't worry if group is small – it's much easier to organise meetings.
- Do writing at every meeting (if you agreed to) – don't just talk about it.

Appendix B: Rhetoric and composition: exposition and argument

Exposition

1   Description

What is it? What are its features (the five senses): sight, sound, look, touch, smell? What are its features (components): first principles, underpinning principles, assumptions, uses, adaptations, implementations? Examples? How contentious is your description? How would others describe this subject? Has anyone else described it in this way? Who? When? Where? Why?

2   Narration

What happened? What was the order of events? How long did it take? Were there episodes along the way? Were some events different from others? Who did what? Why have you selected these events (and not others)?

3   Process

What are/were the steps in the process? What imperative makes/made them happen in this order? What is/was the progression? What are the links between these steps? Why did you choose these steps (and not others)? Why did you choose this progression?

4   Comparison and contrast
   (a) Whole body structure: describe each subject as a whole, break each subject down into parts in the same way, describe similarities and differences.
   (b) Point-by-point structure: describe the parts of each subject, compare each part with corresponding part of the other subject, then repeat with all parts.

   Which mode is better for your subject?

5   Analysis

How does this subject divide up into parts? What does that reveal? What holds the part together? How arguable is your analysis?

6   Classification

How can parts of this subject be grouped? What classification scheme would account for all the parts? What is the principle of division?

7   Definition

A combination of all of the above.

Argument

1   Categorical proposition

What statement do you want to make about the way things are? How contentious is this statement? How much definition do you need to use? Do you have representative examples?

2   Causal analysis

How did things get this way? What is the causal relationship? What is the agency – the mechanism of the causal relationship?

3   Evaluation

How will you define 'good' and 'bad'? Do you have representative examples?

4   Refutation

What are the counter-arguments? What are the reasons for them? Is there any common ground between those and your argument? What are the areas of exclusion?

5   Proposal

A combination of all of the above:

(a) What is the problem? Define with examples. Who else thinks it is a problem? For whom? Where? When? Since when? What are the costs in time, money, people, ethics of doing nothing about it?
(b) What are you proposing? What should be done? Who would do it? How much will it cost? How long will it take? How do you know it is feasible?
(c) How will this solve the problem? What good effects will result: minicausal argument? What are the counter-arguments? Anticipate refutation and counter the counter-arguments. Are there precedents? Are there trade-offs? Are there savings to be made, in any sense?

Appendix C: Academic writing module

Rationale

This module will introduce theoretical frameworks for academic writing, drawing on UK research on academic writing and on the Rhetoric and Composition literature of North American Higher Education. These will be contextualized in participants' academic disciplines. Participants will be encouraged to choose a focus for this module: either their own writing or their use of writing activities in teaching (undergraduate and postgraduate). Processes for monitoring writing development will also be considered.

Aim

To provide participants with frameworks for developing either their writing or for using writing to enhance teaching and learning in specific courses.

Objectives

Course participants will:

* review the purposes and forms of academic writing in their disciplines;
* contextualize frameworks for writing development in their disciplines;
* select aspects of these frameworks to use in their writing and/or teaching; and
* identify sources of strategies for developmental writing and assessment.

Content

1   Overview of approaches to academic writing in the disciplines.
2   Overview of approaches to teaching and researching academic writing in the literature.
3   Models of the writing process: cognitive development, problem solving, discourse, students' conceptions.
4   Productive strategies: freewriting and generative writing.
5   Assessment and development: coherence and criteria.
6   Social processes: peer feedback, writer's groups, collaborative writing, dialogue, emotional processes.

Assessment

Either

(a) A report of 3000 words on a specific teaching innovation, in which the participant introduces or modifies writing activities in a course or part of a course. Key elements of this report:

- course context;
- literature on academic writing which has influenced the innovation;
- aims of the innovation;
- stages in the innovation process;
- specific writing activities involved; and
- evaluation of the innovation.

Participants are encouraged to discuss proposed innovations with the module tutor, with other course participants and with colleagues in their departments at each stage of the project.

Or

(b) Writing for publication: an outline of a paper on a topic of the participant's choice. Key elements of this outline:
- topic and working title;
- the target journal (instructions for authors to be submitted);
- themes and sub-themes;
- outline of the full paper, including length and scope of sections; and
- draft abstract and introduction, time plan for completion.

This assessment will include a descriptive report of 1000 words on the writing process. The length and scope of this assignment will be agreed with the module tutor.

Appendix D: Writing for Publication workshop

Morning

- Introduction
  - o Overview of approaches to writing
  - o Combining different approaches
  - o Targeting and analysing journals and generating text
  - o Defining strategies: 'binge' and 'snack' writing and goal setting

- Writing activity
  - o 5-minute writing: warm-up prompt, with goal setting and discussion

- Overview of prompts for writing
  - o Journal-specific prompts: analysing abstracts
  - o Using verbs to define purpose and develop structure of arguments

- Writing activities
  - o Email to editors with an initial, pre-submission inquiry + discussion
  - o Five minutes freewriting
  - o Five minutes generative writing + discussion and feedback

Afternoon

- Writing activity
  - o Drafting abstract using series of prompts + discussion and feedback
- Overview of outlining
  - o Three levels of outline to include sections and sub-sections and goals
- Writing activity
  - o Sketching an outline of the article + discussion and feedback
- Revising
  - o Strategies and focus
- A process for dealing with reviewers' feedback

- Overview of strategies for the long term
  - o Writing retreats, writing meetings, writer's groups and micro-groups
- Planning
  - o Next writing goals, sub-goals, steps and interim deadlines

Appendix E: Six-month Writing for Publication course

Month 1 Workshop

Getting started	Using prompts and warm ups for writing
Structured discussion	Writing plans, subjects for papers
Targeting	Choosing a journal and contacting editors
Drafting an abstract	Using Brown's 8 questions (Murray, 2013b)
Planning	Interim meetings

Month 2 Workshop

Writing warm-up	Review and discussion – progress and new sub-goal
Strategies	Regular writing, 'snack v. binge' writing
Reporting	Responses from journal editors
Writing time	1 hour (+ discussion)
Goal setting	Specific goals: short, medium and long term

Month 3 Workshop

Writing warm-up	Choose from range of activities
Review	Interim meetings, progress and problems
Analysing	Abstracts of published papers
Analysing	Structure of papers published in target journals
Discussion	Rehearsing arguments

Month 4 Workshop

Taking stock	Progress with writing goals set + re-setting goals
Outlining	Detailed outline, 'calibrated' with target journal
Analysing	Introductions to published papers
Writing time	Using outline

Month 5 Workshop

Review of progress	Counting words written, topics covered
Peer review	How to comment on writing-in-progress
Analysing	Papers published in target journals
Writing time	+ discussion, planning, goal setting for writing

Month 6 Workshop

Reviewers' feedback	Emotional impact, analysing, processing, responding
Peer review	Feedback and revision
Writing time	Completing drafts, peer review, revision
Planning	Goal setting

Appendix F: Structured Writing Retreat programme

Day 1

5.00–5.30 PM	Welcome, introductions, aims and format
	Set up equipment (laptops, cables and printer)
	Writing 'warm-up': five mins writing + ten mins discussion
	Setting writing goals and sub-goals for retreat
5.30–6.30	**Writing session 1**

Day 2

9.15–9.30	Discussion: set writing goals for the day
9.30–11.00	**Writing session 2**
11.00–11.30	Coffee/tea break
11.30–12.30	**Writing session 3**
12.30–1.30	Lunch
1.30–3.00	**Writing session 4**
3.00–3.30	Coffee/tea break
3.30–5.30	**Writing session 5**
5.30–5.45	Discussion: review writing goals, set new goals

Day 3

9.15–9.30	Discussion: set writing goals for the day
9.30–11.00	**Writing session 6**
11.00–11.30	Coffee/tea break
11.30–12.30	**Writing session 7**
12.30–1.30	Lunch
1.30–3.00	**Writing session 8**
3.00–3.30	Coffee/tea break
3.30–4.00	Take stock: goals achieved/not, outputs, feedback
	Reset goals/set new goals

Appendix G: Writing meeting template

Prompt reflection on writing by asking the writer questions. The prompter fills in steps 1–5 for the writer. The writer fills in step 6.

Date of meeting   _____

Name of writer   _____

Name of prompter   _____

Guidance for prompter:

- Sit in a quiet place.
- Adopt an open body position.
- Keep good eye contact with the writer and actively listen.
- Attend, reflect and paraphrase for the writer.
- Have an open, honest discussion.

Step 1: Stage of change

Once you are both settled, ask the writer what stage he/she is in at this time in his/her writing: 'Which of these sounds most like you, right now?'

Contemplation   'I want to write'.

Preparation   'I have done some writing, but not enough'.

Action   'I have been writing, but only recently (less than six months)'.

Maintenance   'I have been writing regularly for some time (six months/more)'.

Stage   _____

Step 2: Decisional Balance

Fill out the following Decisional Balance for the writer. List benefits he/she experiences/anticipates when he/she writes and drawbacks of not writing.

What are the benefits of writing?	What are drawbacks of not writing?

Step 3: Anticipating barriers to writing

Do you anticipate any barriers to your writing?

_____

If so, how will you overcome them?

_____

_____

Step 4: Set realistic, acceptable, manageable and achievable goals.

What is/are your long-term goal(s) for writing?

_____

What is your next realistic short-term goal(s) for writing?

_____

_____

Step 5: Avoiding barriers

Are there times when there are risks that will stop you achieving your goals?

_____

What can you do to avoid that?

_____

_____

The prompter now reviews and reflects with the writer on steps 1–5.

Step 6: Action plan (to be filled in by the writer)

Writer's name _____   Date _____

Check that these writing goals are specific, in real time, realistic, acceptable, manageable and achievable.

My goal(s): short-term _____

My goal(s): long-term _____

_____

_____

Actions I will take in order to achieve these goals:

_____

_____

Date and place of next meeting _____

_____

_____

Bibliography

Acker, A. and Armenti, C. (2004) 'Sleepless in academia', *Gender and Education*, 16(1): 3–24.

Aitchison, C. (2009) 'Writing groups for doctoral education', *Studies in Higher Education*, 34(8): 905–916.

Aitchison, C. and Guerin, C. (eds) (2014) *Writing Groups for Doctoral Education and Beyond: Innovations in Theory and Practice*. Abingdon: Routledge

Aitchison, C. and Lee, A. (2006) 'Research writing: Problems and pedagogies', *Teaching in Higher Education*, 11(3): 265–278.

Aitchison, C., Kamler, B. and Lee, A. (eds) (2010) *Publishing Pedagogies for the Doctorate and Beyond*. Abingdon: Routledge.

Åkerlind, G.S. (2005) 'Academic growth and development: How do university academics experience it?', *Higher Education*, 50(1): 1–32.

Ball, S.J. (2003) 'The teacher's soul and the terrors of performativity', *Journal of Education Policy*, 18(2): 215–228.

Ballenger, B. (2004) *The Curious Researcher: A Guide to Writing Research Papers*, 4th edn. New York: Pearson Longman.

Bandura, A. (1997) *Self-Efficacy: The Exercise of Control*. New York: Freeman.

Barcan, R. (2013) *Academic Life and Labour in the New University: Hope and Other Choices*. Farnham: Ashgate.

Barnett, R. (1999) *Realizing the University in an Age of Supercomplexity*. Buckingham: Open University Press.

Bennett, J.B. (2003) *Academic Life: Hospitality, Ethics and Spirituality*. Bolton, MA: Anker Publishing.

Bereiter, C. and Scardamalia, M. (1987) *The Psychology of Written Composition*. London: Lawrence Erlbaum.

Biesta, G., Allan, J. and Edwards, R. (2011) 'The theory question in research capacity building in education: Towards and agenda for research and practice', *British Journal of Educational Studies*, 59(3): 225–239.

Billig, M. (2013) *Learn to Write Badly: How to Succeed in the Social Sciences*. Cambridge: Cambridge University Press.

Black, D., Brown, S. and Race, P. (1998) *500 Tips for Getting Published: A Guide for Educators, Researchers and Professionals*. London: Kogan Page.

Blaxter, L., Hughes, C. and Tight, M. (1998) 'Writing on academic careers', *Studies in Higher Education*, 23(3): 281–295.

Boice, R. (1987a) 'Is release time an effective component of faculty development programs?', *Research in Higher Education*, 26(3): 311–326.

Boice, R. (1987b) 'A program for facilitating scholarly writing', *Higher Education Research and Development*, 6(1): 9–20.

Boice, R. (1990a) *Professors as Writers: A Self-help Guide to Productive Writing*. Stillwater, OK: New Forums Press.

Boice, R. (1990b) 'Faculty resistance to writing-intensive courses', *Teaching of Psychology*, 17(1): 13–17.

Boice, R. (1992) 'Encouraging scholarly productivity', in *The New Faculty Member: Supporting and Fostering Professional Development*. San Francisco, CA: Jossey-Bass, pp. 160–183.

Bolden, R., Petrov, G. and Gosling, J. (2008) 'Tensions in higher education leadership: Towards a multi-level model of leadership practice', *Higher Education Quarterly*, 62(4): 358–376.

Botshon, L. and Raimon, E. (2009) 'Writing group as sanctuary', *The Chronicle of Higher Education*, May 1.

Brown, R. (1994/95) 'Write right first time', *Literati Newsline*, Special Issue: 1–8.

Butler, J. (1990) *Gender Trouble: Feminism and the Subversion of Identity*. London: Routledge.

Caffarella, R.S. and Barnett, B.G. (2000) 'Teaching doctoral students to become scholarly writers: The importance of giving and receiving critiques', *Studies in Higher Education*, 25(1): 39–54.

Carnell, E., MacDonald, J., McCallum, B. and Scott, M. (2008) *Passion and Politics: Academics Reflect on Writing for Publication*. London: Institute of Education.

Christie, D. and Menter, I. (2009) 'Research capacity building in teacher education: Scottish collaborative approaches', *Journal of Education for Teaching*, 35(4): 337–354.

Clegg, S. (2008) 'Academic identities under threat?', *British Educational Research Journal*, 34(3): 329–345.

Clughen, L. and Hardy, C. (eds) (2012) *Writing in the Disciplines: Building Supportive Cultures for Student Writing*. Bingley: Emerald.

Cresswell, T. (1996) *In Place/Out of Place: Geography, Ideology and Transgression*. Minneapolis, MN: University of Minnesota Press.

Day, A. (1996) *How to Get Research Published in Journals*. Aldershot: Gower.

Deem, R. (1998) 'New managerialism in higher education: The management of performances and cultures in universities', *International Studies in the Sociology of Education*, 8(1): 56–75.

Deem, R. (2005) 'Management as ideology: The case of "new managerialism" in higher education', *Oxford Review of Education*, 31(2): 217–235.

Deem, R., Hillyard, S. and Reed, M. (2008) *Knowledge, Higher Education and the New Managerialism*. Oxford: Oxford University Press.

Donaghy, M. and Morss, K. (2000) 'Guided reflection: A framework to facilitate and access reflective practice within the discipline of physiotherapy', *Physiotherapy*, 16(1): 3–14.

Elbow, P. (1973) *Writing Without Teachers*. Oxford: Oxford University Press.

Elbow, P. (1998) *Writing With Power*, 2nd edn. New York: Oxford University Press.

Elbow, P. and Sorcinelli, M.D. (2006) 'The faculty writing place: A room of our own', *Change*, 38(6): 17–22.

Eley, A. and Murray, R. (2009) *How to be an Effective Supervisor: Best Practice in Research Student Supervision*. Maidenhead: Open University Press.

Emig, J. (1977) 'Writing as a mode of learning', *College Composition and Communication*, 28(2): 122–128.

Fahnestock, J. and Secor, M. (1990) *A Rhetoric of Argument*, 2nd edn. New York: McGraw-Hill.

Flower, L. and Hayes, J.R. (1981) 'A cognitive process theory of writing', *College Composition and Communication*, 32(4): 365–387.

Foucault, M. (1977) *Discipline and Punish: The Birth of the Prison*, trans. Alan Sheridan. London: Penguin.

Geller, A.E. and Eodice, M. (eds) (2013) *Working with Faculty Writers*. Boulder. CO: Utah State University Press

Gere, A.R. (1987) *Writing Groups: History, Theory, and Implications*. Carbondale, IL: Southern Illinois University.

Grant, B. (2006) 'Writing in the company of other women: Exceeding the boundaries', *Studies in Higher Education*, 31(4): 483–495.

Grant, B. and Knowles, S. (2000) 'Flights of imagination: Academic writers be(com)ing writers', *International Journal for Academic Development*, 5(1): 6–19.

Gutkind, L. (ed.) (2005) *In Fact: The Best of Creative Nonfiction*. London: Norton.

Haines, D.D., Newcomer, S. and Raphael, J. (1997) *Writing Together: How to Transform Your Writing in a Writing Group*. New York: Pedigree.

Hargreaves, T. (2011) 'Practice-ing behaviour change: Applying social practice theory to pro-environmental behaviour change', *Journal of Consumer Culture*, 11(1): 79–99.

Hartley, J. (1994) 'Three ways to improve the clarity of journal abstracts', *British Journal of Educational Psychology*, 64(2): 331–343.

Hartley, J. (2004) 'Current findings from research on structured abstracts', *Journal of the Medical Library Association*, 92(3): 368–371.

Hartley, J. (2008) *Academic Writing and Publishing: A Practical Handbook*. Abingdon: Routledge.

Hartley, J. and Branthwaite, A. (1989) 'The psychologist as wordsmith: A questionnaire study of the writing strategies of productive British psychologists', *Higher Education*, 18(4): 423–452.

Hartley, J., Sotto, E. and Pennebaker, J. (2002) 'Style and substance in psychology: Are more influential articles more readable than less influential ones?' *Social Studies of Science*, 32(2): 321–334.

Herrington, A.J. (1992) 'Composing one's self in a discipline: Students' and teachers' negotiations', in M. Secor and D. Charney (eds) *Constructing Rhetorical Education*. Carbondale, IL: Southern Illinois University Press, pp. 91–115.

Hey, V. (2001) 'The construction of academic time: Sub/contracting academic labour in research', *Journal of Education Policy*, 16(1): 33–43.

Higgs, J. and Jones, M. (2000) 'Clinical reasoning in the health professions', in J. Higgs and M. Jones (eds) *Clinical Reasoning in the Health Professions*, 2nd edn. Oxford: Butterworth-Heinemann, pp. 3–14.

Hislop, J., Murray, R. and Newton, M. (2008) 'Writing for publication: A case study', *Practice Development in Health Care*, 7(3): 143–155.

Holligan, C., Wilson, M. and Humes, W. (2011) 'Research cultures in English and Scottish education departments: An exploratory study of academic staff perceptions', *British Educational Research Journal*, 37(4): 713–734.

hooks, b. (1996) *Bone Black*. New York: Henry Holt.

Huff, A.S. (1999) *Writing for Scholarly Publication*. London: Sage.

Hughes, A.R., Gillies, F., Kirk, A.F., Mutrie, N., Hillis, W.S. and MacIntyre, P.D. (2002) 'Exercise consultation improves short-term adherence to exercise during phase IV cardiac rehabilitation: A randomized controlled trial', *Journal of Cardiopulmonary Rehabilitation*, 22(6): 421–425.

Hughes, A.R., Mutrie, N. and MacIntyre, P.D. (2007) 'The effect of an exercise consultation on maintenance of physical activity after completion of phase III exercise based cardiac rehabilitation', *European Journal of Cardiovascular Prevention and Rehabilitation*, 14(1): 114–121.

Ivanic, R. and Lea, M. (2006) 'New contexts, new challenges: the teaching of writing in UK higher education', in L. Ganobcsik-Williams (ed.) *Teaching Academic Writing in UK Higher Education: Theories, Practices and Models*. Basingstoke: Palgrave Macmillan.

Jackson, D. (2009) 'Mentored residential writing retreats: A leadership strategy to develop skills and generate outcomes in writing for publication', *Nurse Education Today*, 29(1): 9–15.

Kahn, W.A. (2001) 'Holding environments at work', *Journal of Applied Behavioural Science*, 37(3): 260–279.

Kamler, B. and Thomson, P. (2008) 'The failure of dissertation advice books: Towards alternative pedagogies for doctoral writing', *Educational Researcher*, 37(8): 507–514.

Kean, A. (2007) 'Writing for publication: Pressures, barriers and support strategies', *Nurse Education Today*, 27(5): 382–388.

Kearns, H. and Gardiner, M. (2007) 'Is it time well spent? The relationship between time management behaviours, perceived effectiveness and work-related morale and distress in a university context', *Higher Education Research and Development*, 26(2): 235–247.

Kirk, A., Barnett, J., Graham, L. and Mutrie, N. (2009) 'Twelve month changes in physical activity and quality of life outcomes following a physical activity consultation delivered in person or in written form in Type 2 diabetes, The TIME2ACT study', *Diabetes*, 58: A97-A97.

Kirk, A., MacMillan, F. and Webster, N. (2010) 'Application of the Transtheoretical model to physical activity in older adults with Type 2 diabetes and/or cardiovascular disease', *Psychology of Sport and Exercise*, 11(4): 320–324.

Klingner, J.K., Scanlon, D. and Pressley, M. (2005) 'How to publish in scholarly journals', *Educational Researcher*, 34(8): 14–20.

Lave, J. and Wenger, E. (1991) *Situated Learning: Legitimate Peripheral Participation*. Cambridge: Cambridge University Press.

Lea, M.R. and Street, B.V. (1998) 'Student writing in higher education: An academic literacies approach', *Studies in Higher Education*, 23(2): 157–172.

Lea, S. and Stierer, B. (2009) 'Lecturers' everyday writing as professional practice in the university workplace: New insights into academic identities', *Studies in Higher Education*, 34(4): 417–428.

Lee, A. and Boud, D. (2003) 'Writing groups, change and academic identity: Research development as local practice', *Studies in Higher Education*, 28(2): 187–200.

Lee, A. and Murray, R. (forthcoming) 'In how many ways can supervisors help postgraduate research students when focusing on academic writing?' *Innovations in Education and Training International*.

Lillis, T. (2001) *Student Writing: Access, Regulation and Desire*. London: Routledge.

Lillis, T. (2009) 'Bringing writers' voices to writing research: Talk around research', in A. Carter, T. Lillis and S. Parkin (eds) *Why Writing Matters: Issues of Identity in Writing Research and Pedagogy*. Amsterdam: John Benjamins, pp. 169–188.

Loughlan, C. and Mutrie, N. (1995) 'Conducting an exercise consultation: Guidelines for health professionals', *Journal of the Institute of Health Education*, 33(3): 78–82.

Lucas, L. (2009) 'Research management and research cultures: Power and productivity', in A. Brew and L. Lucas (eds) *Academic Research and Researchers*. Maidenhead: Society for Research into Higher Education and Open University Press-McGraw-Hill, pp. 66–79.

MacLeod, I., Steckley, L. and Murray, R. (2009) 'Strategic engagement: Developing academic identities through writer's retreat', British Educational Research Association Annual Conference, Manchester.

MacLeod, I., Steckley, L. and Murray, R. (2012) 'Time is not enough: Promoting strategic engagement with writing for publication', *Studies in Higher Education*, 37(5): 641–654.

Marcus, B.H. (1994) 'The transtheoretical model: Applications to exercise behaviour', *Medicine, Science, Sport and Exercise*, 26(11): 1400–1404.

Markland, D., Ryan, R.M., Tobin, V.J. and Rollnick, S. (2005) 'Motivational interviewing and self-determination theory', *Journal of Social and Clinical Psychology*, 24(6), 811–831.

Marshall, J., Coleman, J. and Reason, P. (eds) (2011) *Leadership for Sustainability: An Action Research Approach*. Sheffield: Greenleaf.

Mayrath, M. (2008) 'Attributions of productive authors in educational psychology journals', *Educational Psychology Review*, 20(1): 41–56.

McGrail, R.M., Rickard, C.M. and Jones, R. (2006) 'Publish or perish: A systematic review of interventions to increase academic publication rates', *Higher Education Research and Development*, 25(1): 19–35.

Menzies-Lyth, I. (1988) *Containing Anxiety in Institutions: Selected Essays*, Vol. 1. London: Free Association Books.

Middlehurst, R. (2008) 'Not enough science or not enough learning? Exploring the gaps between leadership theory and practice', *Higher Education Quarterly*, 62(4): 322–339.

Miller, W.R. and Rollnick, S. (1991) *Motivational Interviewing: Preparing People to Change Addictive Behaviour*. New York: Guilford Press.

Miller, W.R. and Rollnick, S. (2002) *Motivational Interviewing: Preparing People for Change* (2nd edn). London: Guilford Press.

Moore, S. (2003) 'Writers' retreats for academics: Exploring and increasing the motivation to write', *Journal of Further and Higher Education*, 27(3): 333–342.

Moore, S., Murphy, M. and Murray, R. (2010) 'Increasing academic output and supporting equality of career opportunity in universities: Can writers' retreats play a role?', *Journal of Faculty Development*, 24(3): 21–30.

Morss, K. and Murray, R. (2001) 'Researching academic writing within a structured programme: Insights and outcomes', *Studies in Higher Education*, 26(1): 35–52.

Moxley, J.M. and Taylor, T. (1997) *Writing and Publishing for Academic Authors*, 2nd edn. London: Rowman and Littlefield.

Mullainathan, S. and Shafir, E. (2013) *Scarcity: Why Having Too Little Means So Much*. London: Allen Lane.

Murray, J. and Pollard, A. (2011) 'International perspectives on research capacity building', *British Journal of Educational Studies*, 59(3): 219–224.

Murray, R. (2001) 'Integrating teaching and research through writing development for students and staff', *Active Learning in Higher Education*, 2(1): 31–45.

Murray, R. (2002) 'Writing development for lecturers: Moving from further to higher education: A case study', *Journal of Further and Higher Education*, 26(3): 229–239.

Murray, R. (2006) 'Reconfiguring Academic Writing', Society for Research into Higher Education Annual Conference, Brighton.

Murray, R. (2007a) 'Incremental writing: A model for thesis writers and supervisors', *South African Journal of Higher Education*, 21(8): 1064–1074.

Murray, R. (2007b) 'Writer's retreat: Reshaping academic writing practices', Society for Research into Higher Education Annual Conference, Brighton.

Murray, R. (2008a) 'Innovations, activities and principles for supporting academics' writing', in S. Moore (ed.) *Supporting Academic Writing Among Students and Academics*, SEDA Special 24. London: Staff and Educational Development Association.

Murray, R. (2008b) 'Moving from peripheral participation to communities of practice: Writer's group in an education faculty', British Educational Research Association Annual Conference, Edinburgh.

Murray, R. (2008c) 'Transforming academic writing practices', Improving University Teaching Conference, Glasgow.

Murray, R. (2008d) 'Writing anywhere, any time: "snacking", "retreating" and "advancing" in academic writing', Keynote Presentation, Writing Development in Higher Education Conference, Glasgow.

Murray, R. (2010a) 'Becoming rhetorical', in C. Aitchison, B. Kamler and A. Lee (eds) *Publishing Pedagogies for the Doctorate and Beyond*. Abingdon: Routledge, pp. 189–213.

Murray, R. (2010b) 'The writing consultation: Developing sustainable writing behaviour', Writing Development in Higher Education Conference, London.

Murray, R. (2011a) 'Engagement with writing for publication/disengagement from other tasks', British Educational Research Association Annual Conference, London.

Murray, R. (2011b) *How to Write a Thesis*, 3rd edn. Maidenhead: Open University Press/McGraw-Hill.

Murray, R. (2011c) 'Performativity or peer-formativity? Academics' responses to research policy and regulation', Society for Research into Higher Education Annual Conference, Newport, Wales.

Murray, R. (2012a) 'Developing a community of research practice', *British Educational Research Journal*, 38(5): 783–800.

Murray, R. (2012b) 'The Social Framework: A model for writing', Writing Development in Higher Education Conference, Liverpool.

Murrray, R. (2012c) 'What is higher education for? Shared and contested ambitions', Society for Research into Higher Education Annual Conference, Newport, Wales.

Murray, R. (2013a) 'It's not a hobby: Reconceptualizing the place of writing in academic work', *Higher Education*, 66(1): 79–91.

Murray, R. (2013b) *Writing for Academic Journals*, 3rd edn. Maidenhead: Open University Press-McGraw-Hill.

Murray, R. (2014) 'Doctoral students create new spaces to write', in C. Aitchison and C. Guerin (eds) *Writing Groups for Doctoral Education and Beyond: Innovations in Theory and Practice*. Abingdon: Routledge.

Murray, R. and Cunningham, E. (2011) 'Managing researcher development: "Drastic transition"?', *Studies in Higher Education*, 36(7): 831–845.

Murray, R. and MacKay, G. (1998a) *Writer's Groups for Researchers and How to Run Them*, Briefing Paper 36. Sheffield: Universities' and Colleges' Staff Development Agency.

Murray, R. and MacKay, G. (1998b) 'Supporting academic development in public output: Reflections and propositions', *International Journal for Academic Development*, 3(1): 54–63.

Murray, R. and Moore, S. (2006) *The Handbook of Academic Writing: A Fresh Approach*. Maidenhead: Open University Press-McGraw-Hill.

Murray, R. and Newton, M. (2008) 'Facilitating writing for publication', *Physiotherapy*, 94(1): 29–34.

Murray, R. and Newton, M. (2009) 'Writing retreat as structured intervention: Margin or mainstream?' *Higher Education Research and Development*, 28(5): 541–553.

Murray, R. and Thow, M. (forthcoming) 'Peer-formativity: A framework for academic writing', *Higher Education Research and Development*.

Murray, R., Steckley, L. and MacLeod, I. (2010) 'Defining the leadership role in enabling academics to manage competing tasks', British Educational Research Association Annual Conference, Warwick.

Murray, R., Steckley, L. and MacLeod, I. (2012) 'Research leadership in writing for publication: A theoretical framework', *British Educational Research Journal*, 38(5): 765–781.

Murray, R., Thow, M., Moore, S. and Murphy, M. (2008) 'The writing consultation: Developing academic writing practices', *Journal of Further and Higher Education*, 32(2): 119–128.

Nagy, J. (2011) 'Scholarship in higher education: Building research capabilities through core business', *British Journal of Educational Studies*, 59(3): 303–321.

Navarra, T. (1998) *Toward Painless Writing: A Guide for Health Professionals*. Thorofare, NJ: Slack.

Ng, L.L. and Pemberton, J. (2013) 'Research-based communities of practice in UK higher education', *Studies in Higher Education*, 38(10): 1522–1539.

Nutley, S., Walter, I. and Davies, H.T.O. (2003) 'From knowing to doing: A framework for understanding the evidence-into-practice agenda', *Evaluation*, 92(2): 125–148.

Obholzer, A. (1986) 'Institutional dynamics and resistance to change', *Psychoanalytic Psychotherapy*, 2(3): 201–206.

Packer, G. (2013) *The Unwinding: An Inner History of the New America*. New York: Faber and Faber.

Peat, J., Elliott, E., Baur, L. and Keena, V. (2002) *Scientific Writing: Easy When You Know How*. London: British Medical Journal Books.

Petrova, P. and Coughlin, A. (2012) 'Using structured writing retreats to support novice researchers', *International Journal for Researcher Development*, 3(1): 79–88.

Pololi, L., Knight, S. and Dunn, K. (2004) 'Facilitating scholarly writing in academic medicine: Lessons learned from a collaborative peer mentoring program', *Journal of General Internal Medicine*, 19(1): 64–68.

Powell. J. and Orme, J. (2011) 'Increasing the confidence and competence of Social Work researchers: What works?', *British Journal of Social Work*, 41(8): 1566–1585.

Reason, P. and Bradbury, H. (eds) (2008) *The Sage Handbook of Action Research: Participative Inquiry and Practice*, 2nd edn. London: Sage.

Reidpath, D.D. and Allotey, P. (2010) 'Can national research assessment exercises be used locally to inform research strategy development? The description of a methodological approach to the RAE 2008 results with a focus on one institution', *Higher Education*, 59(6): 785–797.

Rodrigues, D. (1997) *The Research Paper and the World Wide Web*. Upper Saddle River, NJ: Prentice Hall.

Rose, M. and McClafferty, K.A. (2001) 'A call for the teaching of writing in graduate education', *Educational Researcher*, 30(2): 27–33.

Ruch, G. (2005) 'Reflective practice in contemporary child-care social work: The role of containment', *British Journal of Social Work*, 37(4): 659–680.

Ruch, G. (2007) ' "Knowing", mirroring and containing: Experiences of facilitating child observation seminars on a post-qualification child care programme', *Social Work Education*, 26(2): 169–184.

Rymer, J. (1988) 'Scientific composing processes: How eminent scientists write journal articles', in D.A. Jolliffe (ed.) *Advances in Writing Research, Volume 2: Writing in Academic Disciplines*. Norwood, NJ: Ablex.

Salem, L. and Follett, J. (2013) 'The idea of a faculty writing centre', in A.E. Geller and M. Eodice (eds) *Working with Faculty Writers*. Boulder, CO: Utah State University Press, pp. 50–72.

Selzer, J. (1981) 'Merit and degree in Webster's *The Duchess of Malfi*', *English Literary Renaissance*, 11(1): 70–80.

Sharland, E. (2012) 'All together now? Building disciplinary and inter-disciplinary research capacity in Social Work and Social Care', *British Journal of Social Work*, 42(2): 208–226.

Silvia, P.J. (2007) *How to Write a Lot: A Practical Guide to Productive Academic Writing*. Washington, DC: American Psychological Association.

Spretnak, C. (2011) *Relational Reality: New Discoveries of Interrelatedness That Are Transforming the Modern World*. Topsham, ME: Green Horizon.

Street, B.V. (1984) *Literacy in Theory and Practice*. Cambridge: Cambridge University Press.

Swales, J.M. (2004) *Research Genres: Explorations and Applications*. Cambridge: Cambridge University Press.

Sword, H. (2012a) 'Writing higher education differently: A manifesto on style', *Studies in Higher Education*, 34(3): 319–336.

Sword, H. (2012b) *Stylish Academic Writing*. Cambridge, MA: Harvard University Press.

Thomson, P. and Kamler, B. (2013) *Writing for Peer Reviewed Journals: Strategies for Getting Published*. Abingdon: Routledge.

Thyer, B.A. (1994) *Successful Publishing in Scholarly Journals*. London: Sage.

Toasland, J. (2007) 'Containing the container: An exploration of the continuing role of management in a social work context', *Journal of Social Work Practice*, 21(2): 197–202.

Torrance, M., Thomas, G. and Robinson, E.J. (1993) 'Training in thesis writing: An evaluation of three conceptual orientations', *British Journal of Educational Psychology*, 63(1): 170–184.

Truitt, A. (1982) *Daybook: The Journey of an Artist*. Harmondsworth: Penguin.

Valentine, G. (1998) 'Sticks and stones may break my bones: A personal geography of harassment', *Antipode*, 30(4): 305–332.

Ward, A. (2008) 'Beyond the instructional mode: Creating a holding environment for learning about the use of self', *Journal of Social Work Practice*, 22(1): 67–83.

Waters, L. (2004) 'Scholarship and silence', *Journal of Scholarly Publishing*, 36(1): 15–22.

Wellington, J. (2003) *Getting Published: A Guide for Lecturers and Researchers*. London: Routledge-Falmer.

Wenger, E. (1998) *Communities of Practice: Learning, Meaning and Identity*. Cambridge: Cambridge University Press.

Williams, J. and Coldron, J. (eds) (1996) *Writing for Publication: An Introductory Guide for People Working in Education*. Sheffield: PAVIC.

Zerubavel, E. (1999) *The Clockwork Muse: A Practical Guide to Writing Theses, Dissertations and Books*. Cambridge, MA: Harvard University Press.

Index

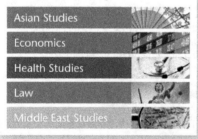

CPSIA information can be obtained
at www.ICGtesting.com
Printed in the USA
LVHW081622110822
725746LV00004B/111

9 780415 828710